Fallen Hero Broken Family

Latarsha Tolson

First paperback edition November 2020

Book design by Guglik Design
Author photographs by Jessica DeLeon
Other credits A huge thank you to Natalie Mangrum for creating the Own Your Story author's cohort, which I was privileged to be part of. And many blessings to the other seven women in my cohort who walked alongside me during this difficult but rewarding process. All my love to you ladies.

ISBN 978-1-735-40530-8 (paperback)
ISBN 978-1-735-40531-5 (ebook)
ISBN 978-1-735-40532-2 (Kindle)

In honor of Humanity

Mom and Dad swore to protect and serve

But with our whole hearts we love our children.

I dedicate to my Beautiful Daughters

Unconditional love and sacrifice for you Always

Love Mommy

Contents

The Text   1

The Detour   15

Breaking the Baby   27

The Shift   39

Early Signs of Trouble   43

Daddy's Girls   67

Preparations   73

The Last Call   99

CHAPTER ONE

The Text

My world was turned upside down on the day that my ex-husband committed suicide. I was married to this man for thirteen years and my greatest fear was getting a visit from clergy to tell me that my husband was murdered by some random encounter, But never did I ever imagine that he would kill himself. I woke up that morning and prepared to take my daughter to school when I noticed that I had a text message. I planned on responding to the message when I had a break in my morning. But before I dropped Deshaun off at school, a call came through. It was, in fact, the same person. I asked if I could call him back in a moment because the tone in his voice was somber. When I disconnected from the call, I immediately said a silent prayer for him because I figured whatever he was calling me about was serious.

Although my intentions were to call him back, I received a call from one of my employees that held my time and attention until I arrived at work. Upon my arrival, I called an emergency meeting with my staff so I did not have time to return his call. During the meeting, I received the call again. As I began to ask him if I could call him back, I paused and asked him if everything was okay. He said it wasn't and he asked me if I was sitting down. He insisted that I do so. I pulled up a stool and assured him that I was sitting and he began with saying that he was sorry. As he spoke, he became emotional and I began to ask him what was wrong. He said, "It's James."

I immediately asked him if James was okay, if something had happened, because he was a Baltimore City Police Officer and my first thought went to a line-of-duty incident. I asked where he was and the voice proceeded to tell me that he was sorry—*James had been shot.* My heart began to beat fast and my palms were sweaty, as I asked him if he was okay and in shock trauma. When I heard the words passed away, I was paralyzed in that very moment. My heart stopped beating and I didn't remember taking a breath at all. Everything around me went dead silent.

Suddenly, the voice on the telephone began to penetrate my hearing and I realized I was talking to someone. I was at a loss for words and all emotion ceased to exist, but I must have said something because my daughter Tyler was standing there with me. I could faintly hear her say, "What about dad? Mom! What happened to my dad?" I just could not speak. I was in such disbelief and it took a minute to process what I was being told.

The gentleman on the telephone told me that it was a self-inflicted fatal shot to the head and that they found him in his home. The more he spoke, the deeper my breathing became and after a while, I began to have chest pain. *No way he was talking about my children's father, because I just spoke with him the other day.* In a split second, I screamed, "Please tell me this isn't true, please! Please! Please! tell me this didn't happen!"

How could this be true? We were planning for our daughter Tara and our grandson to move into his house that Friday. I remember calling him the day before and not getting an answer or a return phone call. It was strange, but I knew he worked a lot so I thought nothing of it. Was this the reason he didn't answer? Indeed, it was.

Before I could begin to process my thoughts, I instantly snapped into mommy mode trying to remain calm, because as I looked into my baby girl Tyler's eyes, I had to muster the strength to tell her that her dad was gone. But I also knew that I couldn't do this. I didn't even have time to digest the news—yet, now I had to say the most horrific words to my daughter. I wish that I had walked away when I answered the telephone so that Tyler wouldn't have heard what happened. But I really didn't think anything of it at the time.

I also knew that there was no way that I could down-play the situation because the horror in her face indeed matched mine. So, I took the deepest breath I could muster and I held her hand and pulled her close to me. My heart was breaking by the second knowing that the words I would speak to her would devastate her to no end. I gently pulled her close to my bosom and held her head to my heart. I embraced her tightly in anticipation of her falling apart. I stroked her hair and kissed her forehead. Perhaps, I was trying to work up the courage to say the words—the words that my mind would not allow me to process—or was I buying time to figure out just what to say. Either way, the last thing I wanted to do was to have to tell my children their dad was dead.

As I was standing in my kitchen with my arms wrapped snugly around her, I whispered the words as softly as I could that her dad was no longer with us. At that very moment she released a gut-wrenching screech and lost all strength in her legs. I gently lowered her to the floor and continued to hold her in my arms. God only knows what I would do to take this pain away—but I was helpless, lost, and broken. I couldn't fix this or take it back and I couldn't make it go away. All I could do was cry out, *"Dear God—WHY?"*

I felt powerless over the situation. Tyler cried out to me with wide eyes, begging me to tell her that it wasn't true. But all I could say was how sorry I was. I sat on that floor for what seemed like an eternity, holding her as she laid in my arms in a fetal position. No words, no sound was coming from her, but she was trembling like a leaf. I coached her through a breathing exercise and told her to sip some water. At first, she refused—but as I encouraged her to focus on me, I was able to lift her from the floor onto the stool. A part of me didn't want to let her go but I needed to, so I asked Theresa, one of my employees, to stay with her while I stepped away.

As I walked out of the kitchen, she grabbed my arm and pleaded that I stay by her side, but I assured her I was not leaving. I just needed to get some air. I walked outside and sat on the front porch. My chest was still tight and by this time, I also had a splitting headache. A rush of thoughts went through my mind because I just couldn't understand how or even why he would do something like this. I mean, he was just here that Friday and today is Monday and he's dead. *Dead!* I can't believe this shit. I had to call Tara because I wanted to tell her before she heard it from anyone else. I must have rung her phone a dozen times before she called me back. I paced that porch like my life depended on it trying to figure out what I was going to say to her. It was hard enough telling Tyler, and I was so scared to tell her. When she did call, I could hear that she was still asleep, so I said to her, "Baby I need you to wake up." I think she noticed that my tone was a bit serious because she asked me if everything was okay. I told her I just needed her to wake up because I had something to tell her. She said okay I am awake, and I then proceeded to break the news to her.

At first, she was quiet and I called her name, but she didn't respond. I said, "Breathe baby—Tara, breathe." At that time, she took a deep breath and I could hear her weeping. All I could tell her was how sorry I felt. I was wrapping my arms around her through the phone. I sat on that phone with her for a moment before I asked her to get dressed and come over to the daycare center. When we got off the phone, I sat there holding my head in my hands because this doesn't get any easier. Although I was able to tell my two older girls, how on earth was I going to tell the baby? Her dad was everything to her, he was her world and of the three, I knew that she would take it the hardest.

I don't remember reaching out to anyone after calling Tara, but my family was notified, because the phone calls were pouring in, one after another. Everyone wanted answers, answers that I didn't have at the time. Someone from my ex-husband's job came to take me downtown and as I was leaving; Tyler came running right behind me. I tried telling her that I would be back soon, but she insisted on going with me because she was in disbelief. The whole ride down she kept asking to go to James' house. She repeatedly said that nothing was wrong with her dad and they made a mistake because he was home and all we must do was go to his house.

That was hard for me. At that time, I really had to reserve my emotion because my baby was surely falling apart. I just sat in the front seat of that car with a blank stare in my eyes. I was numb and speechless. Finally, we arrived downtown and I was a bit nervous because I didn't know what to expect. I had no way of knowing if another bomb was going to be dropped in my lap. Damn! I didn't think this day could get any worse—*but it did.*

As we were being escorted into the police department building, I noticed that there was no one there but us. It felt quite eerie, to be honest. It was cold and dreary. My eyes were very much swollen at the time and everything seemed so hazy. We got in the elevator and when the doors closed, it was like being locked away in a dungeon. The lights were dim, and the silence was so loud that I could hear a ringing in my ears. When the elevator doors finally opened and we stepped out, I had a sinking feeling in my stomach. As we headed down the hall, it was like trying to walk through turbulent waters; it felt heavy. With every step I took toward the closed door ahead of us, I could feel the pressure increasing from my feet to my ankles and up my legs. I held Tyler's hand every step of the way and as we entered the suite she squeezed my hand so tightly that I could tell that she was nervous as well. I gently rubbed my thumb across her hand to comfort her.

There were people in the adjacent offices, but it was so quiet you could hear a pin drop. As we were directed to a specific office, two young ladies greeted us with their condolences and offered us some light refreshments. Though we declined, it occurred to me that I had not eaten breakfast that morning. In fact, I had not eaten anything at all. I hoped that we were not going to be there long but I was told that the representative we were scheduled to meet with would be there soon. While we waited, we were visited by some of his close friends, one after the other, who were in shock and disbelief and they were as shaken up as we were. It was impossible not to cry; the room was filled with a whirlwind of emotions.

This was such a horrific incident, and everyone was beside themselves. No one really knew what to say, because none of us saw this coming. Although I was meeting some of these people for the first time, it seemed that we all were comforting each other, and I was glad to have people sit with us. The officers staggered in, one after the other, expressing their condolences and sharing their grief. It was hard to see but it opened my eyes as to how tragic this loss was for them as well. As a retired police officer myself, I had experienced all too well the fall of a battle buddy and the feelings attached to losing a comrade. Never have I felt it like this. James was not just my children's father, my ex-husband, and my friend—he was a good friend to a lot of people.

A few moments later, Stacie came into the room; she was a close friend of James' and expressed her deepest sympathy. I hugged her because I felt her loss as well. It was very hard to control my tears because there was so much sorrow in the room. She prayed with us and for us and she stayed with us until Michelle, the family affairs liaison, arrived. Michelle came in with open arms and greeted us with the warmest hug. I really needed that because I felt like I was bursting at the seam; that hug gave me the boost to keep it together. I found myself toggling between moments of sadness and moments of strength. I was nervous trying to brace myself for the conversation we were going to have, but Michelle held my hand as she explained why we were there. She carefully asked me if I felt comfortable discussing the details of our conversation with Tyler in the room; I saw no reason not to consent.

I sat there with anticipation, feeling a bit confused and not knowing exactly what to expect, so I just nodded my head in agreement. Michelle went on to explain that because Deshaun is a minor, they had to walk me through the processing of her survivor benefits. She went over some of the documents that her office needed from me and provided detailed instructions for me to make the process easier. I was grateful when she told me that she would be there to help me from start to finish, because this was a lot to take in at one time.

At the end of our conversation, I was emotionally exhausted and very much ready to go and then I was asked questions regarding arrangements for James' services. I told them that I was not sure who would be taking care of that, but I could check with his family to see. I was informed that Deshaun was his legal next of kin and because I was her mother, the responsibility would be mine. I was really confused, and I paused for a second in disbelief, because this didn't make sense to me. I asked if anyone else in his family been notified and they assured me that Natalie and Devlyn his (mom and stepsister) and his Uncle Ronald had been notified at approximately 4:00 in the morning. I was a bit surprised because no one called to tell us in all this time.

My next question was about who stepped in to organize the funeral arrangements for James. I was told no one did at this point, and Uncle Ronald told them he didn't know what to do or anything about what James wanted to be done, which is why my name was given to the medical examiner's office as his next of kin. I was given the telephone number to call to release his body to the funeral home. I was totally beside myself. I wanted so much to decline and walk away because surely someone else should be here. Besides, I had no communication with his family since our divorce 10 years ago. Just as I looked up, Tyler was sitting on the edge of her seat as if she was waiting for me to respond. How could I walk away? I couldn't bring myself to say another word to hurt her, but I also did not feel it was my place to step in. I had so many questions and it seemed that all avenues were pointing at me.

As Michelle was explaining the details to me, I will admit that I checked out a little. I was trying to figure out the next steps that I needed to take to get the ball rolling. The first thing I did was call Natalie, because I wanted to be sure to include James' family in every decision. I know that my children would have wanted to have some input, but it was important to me that everyone was included. Both of his biological parents were deceased and all his siblings, minus one, also preceded him in death. I also had no way of knowing if anyone had reached out to his sister Dominique. I knew that his relationship with her was strained, perhaps I was the best option. I knew that this road would not be easy for many reasons and I was sure to get backlash from his family of how things played out. To be very honest, this was a battle that I didn't want to fight. I didn't want to deal with the back-and-forth headache from either of his sisters when I told them that I was in place to make funeral arrangements.

I never had a relationship with Devlyn, and Dominique is a crazy as they come. So, for good measure, I kept my distance from her through the years. How would they receive this? James had been in a serious relationship with a former coworker of mine—someone with whom we mutually embraced whenever we saw one another. Despite the fact that things were not cohesive between us, Melvina should definitely have a voice as well. I planned to go directly to Natalie's house and talk with her, but I was asked to select the funeral home that would prepare James for services before I left. I didn't have to put much thought into this decision because he and I had spoken in detail about his wishes and I felt that it was best to select a location that was convenient for everyone. Everything was moving so fast; I mean this thing grew legs quickly. —I felt so overwhelmed and somehow, it didn't seem real. It was like I was having an outer body experience.

For a while, I had forgotten that James was dead. Formality and paperwork overtook all emotion and my attention was directed to logistics. If ever I wanted to be someplace else at this very moment, this was that day. Just yesterday, I was having a conversation with my girls about what they were doing for their dad's birthday that coming Sunday. We were brainstorming through gift ideas of things that he liked and what they had gotten him in the past. The joy and the laughter we shared just 24 hours earlier had now imploded with grief and sorrow. Instead of buying him gifts for the celebration of his life, we were faced with organizing arrangements in his memory.

I was exhausted and needed to pause for a minute. The fact that I had not eaten was really taking a toll on me, and I was becoming weak and unable to focus. I asked if we could conclude the meeting so that I could reach out to my family who was having difficulty connecting with me because the phone service connection was poor in the building. Thankfully, my request was honored.

As we were leaving, I stood to my feet and took a deep sigh, Michelle rubbed my back in support, and said that she understood that this was a lot to take in. She also reminded me that although the process was lengthy and difficult, I had the support of the agency, and to call at any time if I needed anything. I was comforted in knowing that the close of this conversation did not mean that I was left to figure this out alone. But that was not why I sighed deeply. I was dreading the thought of telling James' family that I was in place to make decisions on his behalf. I knew that Devlyn was not going to agree, and talking to Dominique was like riding a roller coaster. As I shared this concern, Michelle assured me that if I needed any support when sitting with them, she would be willing to accompany me; all I had to do was ask. Again, a sigh of relief because knowing that she was there for me if I needed support was important.

CHAPTER TWO

The Detour

As we were headed back to the daycare, Tyler insisted that we go to her dad's house, because much like when we were en route to the police department, she believed that he was there asleep. She just did not believe that her dad was dead. I tried to discourage her by saying that no one was able to go to the house now because the homicide unit was probably still there. Unfortunately, that did not matter to her. Despite all my efforts, she insisted that she would go as soon as she returned to her car. That did not sit well with me, so I asked the officer if it was possible to take us to James' house. I absolutely did not want to go, but more importantly, I did not want her to go in there alone. I also knew that there was no way I would be able to prevent her from going because she in fact was the only one with a key to the home.

Although this was once our family home, Tyler and Deshaun both had keys but Deshaun lost her keys just one week earlier. Tyler was living with James until she had moved into her place a few months ago. Although we no longer lived with James, it was home just the same to the girls. So, I knew that if we did not take her that she would have gone on her own, and I did not want that. When we arrived, I sat in that seat and an unsettling feeling came over me. I was surprised to see the front door was closed and there was no yellow tape in sight. There wasn't even a patrol car there, and for a second, I felt a glimpse of hope that this was all a mistake and he really was in the house. I guess a bit of insanity kicked in, because had I not just sat in the office with Michelle for the last three hours discussing what had occurred? In that instant, I snapped out of it. I was so afraid of what was awaiting us on the other side of that door. What were we walking into? Was it messy? Had anyone cleaned up? So many thoughts and fears racing through my mind and body at the same time. I wasn't sure if Tyler could take it; hell, I wasn't sure I could take it. My apprehension was knowing that once we walked inside, we could not unsee what would be before us.

I mustered up the energy to ask Tyler if she was ready and she responded with disbelief. "Yes, because we are going to find him asleep in his bed." We exited the vehicle and she and I held hands as we slowly walked toward the door. It seemed to take us forever to get there. Those steps were like dragging bricks, each step was heavier than the next. She unlocked the door and there was complete silence. I had not been inside this home in almost a year but every time I entered, there was always something going on: whether Peyton, his blue nose pit bull was barking because he wanted some love, or James was cooking and watching sports on the television. Never had I entered this home to find complete silence. It felt wrong. I looked at the officer and silently asked him where the incident had taken place and he mouthed his response to me in the bathroom. I told Tyler to let me go ahead of her. I just wanted to be sure that it wasn't so gruesome that she shouldn't see. I was grateful that she agreed but as I climbed the stairs my stomach sank again.

I began to shake—there was no coming back from this and absolutely no way to prepare myself for what I was about to see. I can assure you—living this moment is nothing like you see in the movies. The air was oppressive and as I climbed each stair, I felt like I was walking through a tunnel. I placed my hands on opposite sides of the paper-peeled walls for support. I could hear the loud thump of my heart's rhythm in my ears. The linen closet was facing the top of the stairs and the doors were removed, and there was no organization of its contents.

When I reached the third step from the top, I turned and looked down the stairs and Tyler and the officer were looking right back at me. So, I turned back and took a deep breath. As I walked up the last three stairs to clear the ledge, I could see that the bathroom door was open. My eyes were stretched as wide as they could; I was trying to take in every detail. It was as if I had never been up those stairs before. I could see that the bathroom door was completely taken off the hinges and propped upside the wall in the hallway. I stood there for a second and looked to his bedroom which was to the right of the bathroom, and sure enough, James was not there. I looked in the bathroom and the first thing I noticed was the vanity mirror was gone, the light was on and the shower curtain was balled up in the sink. At first sight, I thought that someone had cleaned the area because surprisingly, I didn't see any blood. I motioned my arm behind me and placed my hand up for Tyler to stay downstairs and I proceeded to the door. The closer I got, I saw small spatters of blood on the back of the toilet and on the floor. I remember thinking it is awfully clean in here for this to be the location of a suicide. As I moved in closer there were smears of blood on the side of the bathtub, and then *BAM!!* There it was— the bathtub full of blood and matter. I jumped back and took a deep gasp. I quickly put my hands over my mouth to avoid letting them hear me downstairs. Tears began to well up in my eyes and stream down my face as I suppressed my scream. I could not believe what I was seeing. It was in a nightmare.

I turned around and closed my eyes so tightly and, in that moment, Tyler called out to me, "Mommy, can I come up now? Is my dad there?" I quickly gathered myself and wiped my face with the collar of my dress and cleared my throat so I could respond to her. I walked to the top of the stairs and extended my hand to gesture her to come up the stairs. I don't think she touched more than three steps because she got to me so quickly. I asked her if she was sure she wanted to see and she said yes. I moved to the side to allow her to walk ahead of me as I followed closely with my hand around her waist.

She first looked into his bedroom, and I knew instantly what he was thinking. She slowly and cautiously walked into the bathroom and as it became clear to her vision, she turned to me and smothered her face into my chest and screamed, "Daddy, No!!" I held her in my arms and slowly walked her into his bedroom. I could not get her to stop crying; it was like we were pulling the scab off the wound. I tried to comfort her so that we could leave, and she just could not move. Trying to control my own emotions was so hard, but I didn't have time to focus on me while my baby was falling apart.

A few moments passed and she became a little calmer, so I suggested to her that we leave and come back another time. I picked up her keys to escort her out of the bedroom and we noticed three people approaching the house. It wasn't clear to me who it was at first sight, so I told Tyler we needed to go downstairs because we left the front door open. As we reached the bottom of the stairs, the officer was met by the individuals as they entered the home, and Tyler was directly behind him and I followed in the rear.

Devlyn, her Aunt Charlene, and Travis entered the home and were stopped at the door by the officer. Devlyn looked at me as I was standing on the stairs and began to shout, "What the fuck are you doing in my brother's house? Why the hell are you here?" The officer suggested that she calm down and lower her voice. He tried to explain to her the reason we were there, but she did not want to listen. She never took her eyes off me; she was breathing heavily and her face was as cold as steel. Her hands were balled up into fists and she was locked into my eyes with a death stare. She continued to yell, "You shouldn't be in here! How the hell did you get in? Bitch, if you think you are going to get anything that belong to my brother you are mistaken! You ain't getting shit, bitch!" I never said a word and I didn't have to, because clearly, she was putting on a show.

Thankfully, the officer spoke for me so I didn't have to respond to her. Tyler became visibly upset and yelled out with a whimper, "That's my dad!" And Devlyn maliciously yelled at her, "Bitch, he ain't your father! You ain't his daughter!" And then she turned to me and lunged toward me as to try and push pass the officer who was standing directly in front of her and said, "Over my dead body will you get one piece of my brother's belongings! Because you don't know who the fuck you are dealing with! If you haven't heard, bitch, I am rich, and I will make sure you or your fucking kids don't get shit! Try me!" It was difficult for me to stand there and hold my composure while this wild woman, clearly in a vulnerable and emotional state, expressed herself with this level of disrespect toward all of us. Here she stood with the discovery of her brother's death and walked into his home and saw us there—it must have been hard for her to process.

Nevertheless, there was nothing she could do to change the fact that I was there. and surely her actions confirmed exactly how I thought she would respond to my presence. But this is where my law enforcement training kicked in. There was no need to blow up or respond to her gestures or comments because there was an officer present. And I was also too far up the stairs for her to reach me so there was no need for defense. If anything, she would be the one taken into custody for her threats and actions. I also knew that I needed to remain calm for Tyler, because not only was she dealing with her father's death, she was also disrespected by the humiliating comment that James was not her father. I had to focus on what was important at the time, and that was to comfort my child. I pulled her close to me and placed my hands on her face so that we could lock eyes and I said to her, "Pay no attention to her. You know that James is your dad and there is nothing anyone can do about that. You do not have to respond to her." She looked me in the eyes and as the tears flowed down her cheeks, she asked me why Devlyn would say something so hurtful. James was her dad and I assured her that the opinions of others did not matter. I told her, "You know how much your dad loved you and I know how much you loved your dad, and no one not anybody can change or take that away from you."

I stood on those stairs and held her in my arms, while the officer told them that we were leaving and asked them to step out of the house so that we could lock up. Devlyn said that she needed to give me the keys. The officer assured her that we would not surrender any property to her that did not belong to her, and she completely disregarded what he said. She insisted that we give her the keys so that we would have no access to the house. I looked at her like she was crazy, with a smirk on my face—but I still didn't say a word. I was flabbergasted by her demand, because she had not set foot in that house more than two times including that day since we moved in August of 1999. We moved into that house when Tyler was two years old and not one time did she come over for dinner, an event, to visit or even socialize. So, who in the fuck was she to tell my child, who grew up in this house, to give her anything? In fact, if she had a real relationship with her brother, she would have asked Tyler how she was doing and embraced her in comfort. Death brings the worst out of people, everybody is worried about what someone else has as if they are entitled to some shit. Shit—that's all they see is his shit. We didn't care what was in the house or who was going to get what.

We had every right to be in that house on this day or any other day. This was the house that my ex-husband gifted me as a wedding present, and we got married four months after settling in. This was the home where we raised our three beautiful daughters. Although I moved out in 2009, I still had items in our storage space and my children visited their dad quite often. Tyler lived with her dad until she moved into her own apartment. We had every right to be there. The real issue was that she didn't have keys and wanted to get her hands on those so that we didn't have access to the house. The thing that sur-prised me the most is she felt that she had any right to be there and take possession over anything. My children had many comforts of home there and it was my hard-earned money that furnished the house with James before our separation. It was unacceptable—the nerve of anyone to question who, what, where, or why as it pertained to my children and me.

As the officer insisted that they step out of the house so that we could lock up, Devlyn and her best friend stood on the front stoop waiting for us to exit. Because of her irrational behavior, the officer asked that they move away from the house while we exited the home. Devlyn said they could leave and assured the officer that she wouldn't hit me. I stopped in my tracks and gave her a look of death insinuating that I know she wouldn't. She really didn't want this in her life.

In the thirteen years that James and I were together, I had never exchanged not so much as one harsh word or experience with anyone in his family. So I'm not sure who Devlyn thought she was but it was clear that she had no idea who I was. If she thought for a second that she could so much as touch me, she was wrong. Baby! I would have been on her like flies on shit. As she began to respond, the officer addressed the three of them firmly and told them to step over this way without moving until we got into the vehicle. He advised that if they did not follow his instructions, someone would be arrested. They all agreed that they were going to stay as they were instructed, and the officer opened the storm door and instructed Tyler and I to exit. He stood on the outside of the door and held it open and stood as a barrier between us and them and I exited the house first.

Tyler came out after I did and I handed her the keys to lock up the house and Devlyn asked again about who had given me the keys to her brother's house—and demanded that I should give them to her. The officer looked at her and interrupted her—"Ma'am! I already told you that she will not surrender her keys to you. If you have keys of your own, no one can stop you from entering the home, but you will not take possession of these keys." So, we locked the front door and Tyler, in her haste to leave, did not lock the storm door. We walked toward the car and the officer unlocked the doors for us by remote as he lagged to ensure that we safely entered the vehicle. Before we left, Devlyn called the detective that notified them earlier of James' death and he came to the house. He asked for my name and telephone number and said that he wanted us to go ahead to our destination and he would call me after he spoke with them.

As we drove away, I was so angry. How in the hell was I supposed to have a conversation with these people regarding funeral arrangements? It would never happen, especially after what I just experienced. I knew it would be impossible. At that moment. I took matters into my own hands and did what was best for my children. Which was to honor their dad. Tyler was as furious as I was, and she was ready to fight. You know those youngsters are always on go time. She said mom she is lucky you held on to me because I don't play when it comes to you. She could have said anything to me but the way that she acted toward you made me want to jump around that officer and bang her in the face. Then she looked at the officer with a smile and said no disrespect to you Sir, but that's my mom. I reminded her that sometimes we must reserve ourselves, when others lose control. I reminded Tyler that I could have easily met her where she was, but that would have landed us both in cuffs, having to answer to emotions—so I decided to move in silence. And that was how we were going to conduct ourselves—as ladies. We didn't have to respond or answer to anyone; we would move in silence and let our actions speak for us. It would be difficult but that is exactly what we would do.

CHAPTER THREE

Breaking the Baby

I realized how my training had impacted my life—because I can be a hot head and the level of restraint I exercised today. Baby: let me tell you that was Devine intervention at its best. I was thankful to be able to demonstrate to my children a great example of composure.

We arrived at the daycare and the officer extended his condolences again and reminded me that I could call Michelle if I needed anything. We both said thank you and exited the vehicle. As we approached the house, my telephone began to ring nonstop; it was my mom, my boyfriend, my sister, and so on. I returned each call in order of priority; not that they all weren't important, but I slowed down this process to do my best and update everyone. There was something more pressing that I needed to give my attention to at the moment, and that was how I was going to tell my daughter Deshaun the news. I had only a few hours to figure it out because she would be getting out of school soon. I didn't interrupt her day because I knew the coming days would not be easy for her.

I remember Michelle saying that the agency offered us free counseling, so I called and ask her for that information. The therapist called me in the matter of minutes, and I was grateful because I needed help with this one. I asked her how to tell Deshaun that her dad had passed, and she asked me a few questions about Deshaun. She said the best way to tell her was to just to be honest. Deshaun was old enough to take it and no matter what I decided, it would not change her feelings. My heart sank because I had no idea what to say to her, but what I knew was this wasn't going to be easy.

I called my mom back and asked her if we could come to her house when I tell her, and she agreed. Whatever you need, I am here. I asked her if she would reach out to my sibling and ask them to be there as well, and she also agreed. I hung up the telephone and sat back in my chair and let out a deep sigh. My head was pounding and my ears began to ring again, An overwhelming feeling was overcoming me. I wanted to break this news to her this way for two reasons: 1) Because I needed her to be surrounded by her village of loved ones as she received the most devastating news of her life; and 2) I needed support in having to tell her, because I knew I was not strong enough to do it alone. This was too much; it felt as if this nightmare would never end. I was beginning to feel sick to my stomach and then realized that I still had not eaten. I was hungry, exhausted, and weak all at once.

I asked somebody could they please get me something to eat, but that fell on deaf ears because we all were going through it. My employees, Deshaun's godmother, and her employees were all over the place. The mental and emotional impact of the day had exhausted us all—yet, we still had to operate the business. I was so grateful to have so much emotional support at the daycare center because honestly, I don't know how I would have been able to do any of this without them. I asked Deshaun's godmother if she would pick her up from school and bring her to my mother's house. I didn't know how long it would take her to get there by bus and I knew that I was in no condition to drive. I did not want to alarm her that anything was wrong so I thought it was best to have her picked up and brought over by someone else. She agreed to do so, and we all convoyed over to my mother's house.

I arrived maybe an hour before school let out and shortly after I received a call from the detective. He asked if he could meet with me so I invited him to come to my mother's house which was perfect because she lived closer to James' house. He arrived within a few minutes, I invited him in and offered him a seat. He extended his condolences to the family. He was very mild mannered and calm—he presented himself well—but above all, he was very observant of my behavior and the energy of the environment.

He said before I get into the discussion with Devlyn, let me ask how are you doing? I looked at him as the tears welled up in my eyes and said I honestly didn't know. He said that is understandable, and I am sorry for your loss. He said to me that he had spoken with Devlyn at her mother's house earlier that morning when she received the news of her stepbrother's passing. He said that he did not know how things escalated between us, but it was very clear to him what was taking place. I agreed with him because I had no idea why things escalated either. We all are grieving the same loss. He said he could see exactly what was going on. Judging from my demeanor and my family it was clear that we all loved James and our hearts were in the right place. He also said that he could tell that Devlyn's rage was based on material possessions which is something common that occurred during times like these.

He was so kind to share with me his own personal experience when his wife committed suicide—he was the one who found her. It was easy for him to see the difference between hurt and greed. He assured me that he was able to express some truths to Devlyn regarding our presence in the home with the hope that we would experience no further confrontation. I thanked him for taking the time out of his day to follow up with me, and I pray this is behind me as well.

The next half hour seemed to be the most intense; I was on pins and needles as each of my family members arrived. I could not gather myself to relax at all. My boyfriend held me close and hugged me with the desire to comfort me. Although it felt safe and warm, it did not work. I was too on edge and concerned with how I would tell Deshaun. I received play-by-play text messages from her godmother from the time she picked her up from school until she pulled up to the house.

The closer she got, the more I panicked. I must have paced the hardwood floors so much that I could have worn off the finish. *I was a mess.* I couldn't think of how or what to tell her. I moved from one chair to the next trying to find the perfect place to sit. Everyone was standing around looking at me, because they knew I was a wreck and there was nothing they could do to help. I sat down on the sofa's edge and cupped my fist to my mouth and tears welled up in my eyes and rolled down my cheeks as my legs shook uncontrollably. Waiting for her to walk through the door. I could hear the car door shut; you could hear a feather drop inside the house, it was that quiet. It seemed that everyone was bracing themselves for Deshaun's arrival, trying not to cry, look sad or worried. But how can this be, with heavy hearts they stood in solidarity—embraced and supported me with long stares.

The time had come. Deshaun walked onto the porch getting ready to enter the living room. She opened the door and walked in with the biggest smile on her face. She ran to me and yelled "mommy" in the happiest voice, as she always does. She had such an amazing day and wanted to tell me all about it. I tried to perk up and receive her as well. I immediately stood up and hugged her so tightly; I knew she felt that something was different. There I was again! I longed for an exit, wishing that I didn't have to follow through with this. I was afraid to say it. I knew she was going to take it the hardest and I just wasn't ready to tell her.

I looked at her, told her that I loved her, and caressed her face as I stared into her eyes. She asked mommy are you okay, what's wrong? I tried to hold back my tears, but they streamed down my face as I guided her to take a seat. She said, "Mommy, you are scaring me!." I held her hand in mine and wrapped my arm around her shoulders to embraced her. I said calmly, "Baby I have to tell you something." At that time, she looked around at everyone else's faces and then back at mine and said what is it. I told her that I was sorry to have to tell her that her dad died. She looked at me and her eyes began to widen—she was in total disbelief and shock. For a second, she was quiet. I then pulled her close to me and whispered for her to breathe. She exhaled the most painful screech from within her being. She began to shake uncontrollably and yelled out, "Nooooooo!!! This isn't happening!!! Not my dad!" I just caressed her hair and said I know baby. I am so sorry.

She jumped up and ran toward the front door, but no one would let her out so she decided to go up the stairs. She went into the bathroom and I followed her. When I got to the top of the stairs, I could not hear anything so I gently knocked on the door and ask her if I could come in. She did not answer, so I knocked again. I called out to her and said I was coming in and as I turned the knob, I discovered that she locked the door behind her. I asked her to unlock the door. She just wanted to be left alone. Mommy please let me be alone. I understand that you want to be alone right now, but I really needed to see her face to make sure that she was okay so I asked her again, baby please unlock the door. She did. When I stepped into the bathroom, she was balled up in a fetal position with her arms wrapped around her legs, rocking back and forth. I closed the door behind me and slowly eased myself on the floor in the kneeling position in front of her and embraced her. I positioned myself against the bathtub and eased my way beside her and held her as she buried her face into my chest and wept like a baby. I know exactly what she was feeling because my father had died just three years ago.

So there we were sitting on that bathroom floor—both of us fatherless daughters. My heart connected with hers so deeply because I loved my daddy and the fact that he died when I was 41 years old did not make it any easier than her losing her dad at 14 years of age. I could say to her I understand, because I remembered how you all comforted me in my season of loss and as I said this to her, she embraced me. She quietly asked me mom, and I responded gently yes baby. Do you think I could just be alone? I said of course you can, but can you promise me that you will leave the door unlocked and wouldn't stay too long? She agreed. I kissed her forehead and hugged her tightly once more before getting up from the floor. I opened the door and looked back at her and said I love you, and she whimpered, "I love you too, mommy." I softly closed the door behind me and gently rested my body against it on the other side. I melted in that place and fell apart because I could feel her loss, her pain and heartache. And I could not take it away. I hung my head and allowed the tears to fall to the floor and silently said a prayer for my children.

Dear God, Father, I come to you in this hour asking for your forgiveness of my sins. Thank you, God, for my beautiful babies, but most of all, thank you for the amazing dad that you blessed them with. I am before you with the heaviest heart pleading the blood of Jesus over my babies, that you wrap them in your loving arms and rock them in your peace. Please strengthen them when they are weak and comfort them in their brokenness. I know that this way we all shall go, but I pray father, God that I am enough to carry them through this pain. In the moments of lonesomeness comfort, them, in the moments of brokenness, heal them and the moments of pain give them peace. Father, I pray you have mercy on James' soul for his suffering must have been great. And help us to not lean on our own understanding, but to have a heart of forgiveness in the days to come. Father, all of this I pray in your name, Jesus, strengthen me through this journey as well. It is in your perfect peace I pray. Amen.

I opened my eyes, wiped my face, and placed my hand on the door as I walked away, wanting to hold on to her but knowing that I had to let go at the same time. I sat on the top stoop and awaited the door to open. I called out to her after a while to ensure that she was okay. She did not respond so I sent my niece in to check on her. She did honor her word and left the door unlocked and she did not resist her cousin entering the bathroom with her. I could hear them talking in a low tone and when I could hear that she was okay, I went downstairs. When I hit the bottom of the stairs, I took a deep breath and told everyone that she was calm, and one by one, they hugged me and assured me that I did well. There was no easy way or perfect time to say what I had to say, but I was thankful that my family was able to drop everything and be there for us.

I sat on the sofa and laid my head back and my mom gave me a cold wet washcloth and placed it over my eyes to release the pressure. Suddenly, Deshaun slowly emerged from upstairs and asked me if she could stay the night with her godmother. Originally, I said no, because she should be home with us. I needed to make sure she was going to be alright, and if she needed anything, I wanted to be there for her. But she insisted that I let her go. I told her that I thought that she should wait a few days before she stayed the night out. She begged me, mommy please, I just want to be around people and not alone. So, against my own judgment, I agreed only if that was okay with her godmother.

I felt badly that I dumped this on her godmother's lap but I was secretly hoping that she would encourage her to stay home, but as she said she needed to be around other people and at home it was just the three of us and she in fact would have been alone. Her godmother allowed her to come over and I told her that if she needed me to come and pick her up, I would. Before they left, Deshaun pulled me aside and asked if I know how he died. I was caught off guard and I really didn't know what to say. I struggled with what to say. Should I tell her exactly how it happened or should I spare her the gory details? I played it safe and told her that I didn't have all the details and that as soon as I found out I would let her know.

I eased into the kitchen to call the therapist back and ask if I should tell her how James died, and she said something that made perfect since. She advised me to Just tell her without sparing any details. It was more important for her to heal with the truth than with a lie, only to discover the truth later. The therapist was right so I called Deshaun into the kitchen and told her that I just received a called and was told how her dad died. She stood there with her hands clasped and braced herself, she took a deep breath and said okay I am ready. I told her he committed suicide, and she let out a deep sigh. I paused for a moment because I wasn't quite sure how she was going to process this, but It was like she expected me to say that. I asked her if she was okay and she said yes. Then she paused and said, Mom can I tell you something? I said sure baby, she told me that she wasn't really surprised that I said it was suicide because dad hadn't been acting like himself for a while. I know it is hard to hear that he committed suicide, but I honestly thought he may have had a heart attack or died in his sleep. She went on to say that she was glad that he wasn't suffering anymore. I just hugged her. My baby girl had gone from crisis to courage in a matter of minutes. I was taken aback at how strong and mature she was in that moment. I knew that less was more, so I didn't say one more word.

They left shortly after, and as the evening fell, I was left with having to take care of one more order of business. I called the funeral home to schedule an appointment to come in and they gave me an appointment for the next morning. Everyone eventually left and my mom sat with me for a long time. She placed herself on the chair beside me and held me in her arms and whispered to me that I didn't have to be so strong all the time; it was okay to cry. I rested my head in her lap and wept, and for the first time I cried my own tears.

CHAPTER FOUR

The Shift

I was sad and confused because I just could not understand how or why James would do something like this. I reflected back on the last time when I saw him. It was that Friday and he was dropping off Tara and our grandson at the daycare. We talked briefly as we always do, and nothing seemed out of place. I joked with him about playing pop-pop while he was hovering over our grandson as Tyler took him out of the car. He looked at me with a big smile on his face and said yeah. He always dragged that word when he smiled. I asked him how everything was going with preparing the room for Tara and our grandson to move in the following Friday, which happened to be two days before his birthday.

He replied I mean it's alright everything is coming along. I asked him if he needed anything he said he was good. I told him to let me know if anything changes. and he looked at me and said, "Well actually," and he paused and said, "Never mind." I said what is it, and he said nothing. It's all good, I got everything covered. I replied, okie dokie. And he walked toward the car. I was loving on my grandbaby as Tyler was taking him in the house and when I looked up James was standing in the open door of his car that was parked on the driveway looking at us. He looked like he had something on his mind but he didn't say a word—he just had a look. I said let me get back in here and we will catch up later. He said okay and got in his car and backed off of the driveway. When he put his car in drive, he beeped the horn and rolled the window down and waved as he always did with a big smile on his face. We all turned around and waved back. *And that was the last time I saw him alive.*

Looking back at this moment, a million things went through my mind. *That was his goodbye! Is this what he was going to tell me and decided not to say?* I could usually pull it out of him whenever I knew something was bothering him. It didn't matter if we were on the telephone or in person, I knew. We just had that connection. I was wrecking my brain trying to recall if he was struggling with anything but I couldn't come up with anything that made sense. Whenever he seemed down, I would ask him if he was okay and he would always reply with that dragged-out "yeah"—but I knew he wasn't, so I'd ask him what was going on. Let's talk about it. Sometimes, he would complain about his job and how he had one run in after the next with his Sergeant, and I would always encourage him to go for promotion so that he could be the one to make a difference. He would say nah, I don't really want to, and then other times, he would express how heartbroken he was about how Devlyn and Natalie handled his father's arrangements. He felt like they shut him out of everything and did not allow him to be a part of the planning process. He said they knew that he was his father's only son, that they acted like he didn't even matter.

The one thing that hurt him most, and we talked about it so often, was the fact that he wanted his father's car. I asked him if he had a conversation with Natalie about it and he said he didn't want to bother her or overwhelm her with anything. He wanted to wait and see what she wanted to do with it. Well that day never came because I remembered the day he called me crying. He said you wouldn't believe what happened! I said what? He said they had sold his father's car behind his back! I was like what! Are you serious! Did you know they wanted to sell it and he said no! Devlyn knew he wanted that car because he told her. He knew she was behind that mess. That was the one thing he really wanted of his dad's. I always encouraged him and reminded him that he was going to be okay, and tried to give him a word of encouragement to lift his spirits. Even when he expressed how much he missed his dad, I reminded him that he was a good son and his father knew how much he loved him. James was no stranger to grief and heartbreak; but even when he was going through tough times, we talked. I guess this time, he didn't want to talk about it, and maybe he didn't want me to know whatever it was that was bothering him.

CHAPTER FIVE

Early Signs of Trouble

Looking back, there were also signs that Deshaun was struggling and may have suffered from the very depression that challenged James. One day, she came home from spending almost a week at James' house and said that she wanted to tell me something. She was very shaken and scared to say whatever it was. It made me pause a bit, so I centered myself and told her that she could tell me whatever it was. I even joked and asked if she had snuck a boy in her dad's house and got caught. She shook her head and didn't know how to tell me. She became very quiet and tears began to roll down her face; I knew this was serious. I pulled in my chair close, sat in front of her, and held her hand. I looked into her eyes and ask her what was wrong, and she slowly pulled the long sleeve of her sweater up and revealed to me cuts on her forearm. I immediately placed my hand over her arm to cover it up so that no one else in the room could see and told her to go upstairs in my bedroom, that I would be there in a second. When she went upstairs, my heart jumped out of my chest. I could not believe what I had seen, and I could not believe that this was real. I gathered myself for a second and asked God to give me the right words to say to her because I was so lost.

I went upstairs and as I entered my room; she was sitting on my bed. I walked right over to her and hugged her so tightly. I told her that everything was going to be okay and that I was so proud of her. I was so happy that she had the courage to speak out and say something. I continued to hold her, and I began to pray over her. She was so emotional, and I can feel the weight of her secret parting from her body as she lay there in my arms. I knew that I had to tell James so I motioned her up and asked her if she could share this with her dad. She hesitantly said no and I told her that there was no way that we could keep this from him. This was an example of something that parents had to share with one another.

I told her that she didn't have to be the one to tell him and if she wanted me to break it to him, I would do so. I would reassure him that she would talk to him about it when she was ready. She agreed to let me tell him. I kissed her on her forehead and held her for a bit longer. I asked her if I could see her arm again so she pulled up her sleeve.

I noticed that the cuts were on the surface and already scabbed over; they were new but not fresh. I gently rubbed my hand over the cuts and asked her what made her do this. She originally said she didn't know. I asked her what she was thinking about that made her decide to cut herself, and she said she was trying to make the pain go away.

I continued to caress her scars and asked her to explain what do she meant about making the pain go away. She explained that she had these thoughts that made her feel really sad. Sometimes, she could quiet the voices. However, this time, she couldn't so she thought that if she cut herself it would stop the pain. I asked her when and where she did this. She replied that it was two days ago when she was at her dad's. I asked her where her father was, and she said he was at work. She was home alone and when she was getting ready to commit to the attempt, he called to check on her and he told her that he loved her and would be home soon. That made her stop. I asked her if he noticed anything different when he got home. She said no, but he did question the drops of blood on the bathroom floor and on the towel that she used to clean up with.

I asked her what she told him, and she said that she had a nosebleed. I was stunned— I mean this was mind blowing. This was the first time that I heard of voices and thoughts; I never imagined learning that my baby was going to *COMMIT SUICIDE!* She mentioned that she felt a kind of relief because she told me. I kissed her forehead told her I loved her and thanked her for trusting me. I sent her to the medicine cabinet to get the Mederma ointment and showed her how to nurse her scars. I explained to her that it was a possibility that they would not go away completely but this ointment would minimize the scars.

She was quite exhausted, so I told her to lay down for a while and take a load off. In reality, I was really the one who needed to take a load off. I told Tyler that I was leaving for a while and ask her to keep an ear out for Deshaun; I would return shortly. I got in the car and pulled off. I didn't have any particular place to go but I needed some space. I parked my vehicle around the corner, and I screamed as loudly as I could. I needed to release my emotions because I had to suppress them the whole time that I spoke to Deshaun. I didn't want her to know that I was upset, hurt, or even angry at her, because I was not angry at all. I was *scared*.

I didn't know what to do so I called James. He didn't answer right away so I called my boyfriend. We talked for a while and I told him that I needed to see him. I did not want to share this with him over the phone, so we agreed to meet before he came home from work. As I was driving to the location I called my Sissy. I knew that she would be the perfect person to talk to about this. We had always talked about everything, so it was second nature to call her. I think she was as stunned as I was; the more details I shared the more she gasped. I told her I didn't know what to do and she suggested that I take her to the emergency room if I thought she would continue to self-harm.

It was something about these new words that I was hearing *SELF-HARM, COMMIT, THOUGHTS,* and *PAIN.* This was a lot to take in and to be honest I did not know what her state of mind was at the time. So I decided that I would take her to the emergency room. I ended the call when I met up with my boyfriend and I shared the details of the evening with him. He was perplexed and taken back by it all. He was sad that she was struggling like this and so supportive of everything. He had such a big heart for children and there wasn't anything that he would not do for them. I knew that he would respond this way. I told him that I was going to take her and I was going to reach out to James again. He kissed me and told me to let him know if I need anything.

I called once again when I got into the car and this time, James answered. I told him that I needed him to meet me at the emergency department because Deshaun had cut herself. He couldn't believe it! He yelled she did what! I explained to him that she had cut herself at his house with an old razorblade and had told me today when he brought her home. You could hear a pin drop on the phone because he was at a loss for words. James, are you okay, and he cleared his throat and said in a low voice yeah I am alright. He asked where she was and I told him I was on my way to the house to pick her up; he agreed to meet us there. When I got to the house, Tyler had taken Deshaun with her to get a bite to eat. This was good because I needed to explain why she was going to the hospital.

When they pulled up, I met them at the front door, and I told Deshaun to grab her food and bring it with her. I walked toward the car and told her to come with me. When we got in the car, I told her that I needed to take her to be evaluated tonight, and that her dad was on his way to meet us there. She seemed scared, and I can imagine she would be because I am sure she didn't expect this—neither did I. When we pulled into the parking lot, James met us at the hospital entrance and greeted Deshaun with the biggest hug. The look on his face was nostalgic and that of a worried father. You could tell he was all over the place and didn't know what to say.

We went inside and while we were waiting to be called, he kept looking down at the floor with his fingers inter-twined and his jaw was so tense you could see the knots moving up and down. We didn't sit in the waiting room too long before they escorted us to the treatment room. When we arrived, on the outside it looked like every other room but inside this room was different. It had its own restroom and an observation room inside. Deshaun was not allowed to have any of her personal items, not even her food. But because she was a minor, we were allowed to be with her, and she was allowed to eat her food as long as one of us was there with her. They explained that because she had evidence of self-harm, she needed to stay overnight and she would be evaluated in the morning. I asked if we could stay with her and they allowed only one of us to stay. I decided to stay, but I asked James if he could stay there with her until I got back. I wanted to go home and shower and get some clothes for us both for tomorrow and some sleepwear for the night. He hesitantly agreed to stay and he felt that she should be allowed to go home and return in the morning. He was having a real hard time with this.

The hospital was not far from where we lived and right at the halfway point of both of our houses. So it didn't take me long to return. When I came back, Deshaun was undressed and in the bed, and James said that he would return early in the morning in time to see the psychiatrist. He kissed her on her forehead and told her he would see her in the morning. Before he left, he asked me to step out of the room for a moment and I told Deshaun I would be right back. I actually walked him through the emergency department toward the front door. As we walked he said that he didn't understand how this could have happened, I mean she didn't say anything to me about this. He asked me how she shared the news with me and I told him she simply told me. He shook his head and couldn't understand how this happened—we raised her right and we told her that we loved her all of the time. Why did this happen to our baby?

I told him James don't beat yourself up about this; it wasn't something that we did to her. This was something that she experienced and unfortunately, it had become too much for her to deal with and resulted in this suicide attempt. I reassured James that we did everything as parents to encourage, uplift, and love our babies. This was just something we had to push through for Deshaun. I took James' hand and told him that we got this, because she had the both of us in her corner and so much more support than we could ever ask for. I believed that she would be fine.

James took a deep sigh and wiped a tear from his face and said I guess you're right. I wanted to get back to Deshaun so she wouldn't be alone too much longer, I will see you in the morning. As daybreak came, there he was walking through the doors, and just in time because the therapist walked right in behind him. Deshaun and I had talked a while the night before, and surprisingly, she was calm and chatty. We even cracked a few jokes and I made sure she knew that she was not broken but we just wanted to make sure that we do everything that we can to help Deshaun pull through this.

Deshaun said mom I am glad that you are here with me—you made me feel safe. I kissed her forehead and tucked her in for the night. The next morning, the psychiatrist came in and explained to us that they were going to evaluate her and described what that looked like. They asked her a lot of questions to see where she was mentally and emotionally. She was a bit standoffish in the beginning and I asked her if she would please open up to them so that they could help her most effectively. She began to speak, and we were relieved to learn that she did not need to be admitted. They recommended outpatient therapy as they did not see a need for her to be placed on any medication therapy. However, they did suggest that she take a few days off from school.

On the way home, I went to the school to collect her assignments so that she didn't fall behind. I continued to check in on her and speak with James from time to time with updates on her progress while trying to find a therapist that accepted commercial insurance. This was more difficult than I thought, as even the referrals from the insurance company did not have any available appointments. I decided to reach out to my therapist and schedule an appointment with her. Thank God I did because I was running out of options. When I scheduled the appointment I called James and told him that we both had to be present. I gave him the date and time, and he said that he would be there.

So here we were, day one of therapy— and what do you know I called James and he didn't answer my calls. This was quite unusual because we rarely played phone tag. But all of a sudden we were in this cat-and-mouse game. When Deshaun and I had arrived at the appointment, James called and said he was not going to make it because he was just getting off of work. I told him in my "nice/nasty" voice that I didn't care where he was—he needed to find himself at this appointment because he knew that we both had to be there today. I didn't know how far he had to drive but by the time we entered the safe space and sat down, he had walked in the office. He sat there on the edge of his seat, very uncomfortably, and we were asked questions about our family history. He seemed a bit hesitant to say that his mom suffered with depression and his sister Dominique with bipolar disorder. You could tell he really did not want to be there, but it didn't matter because to me this was all about Deshaun.

As the weeks went by, I called James to give him a progress update about every appointment Deshaun had. However, I had taken notice that James never called to ask me how she was doing. So I decided that I would ask him about it. When I did, he said well he really didn't feel that she needed to see a therapist every week like this. She was smart and intelligent, and believed that she could do anything that she put her mind to. I said indeed all of these things are true, but none of these things had anything to do with what she was going through. I told James that I needed him to step in and help me more with getting her around. He flipped out on me as if I said something wrong. He went on to say that his work schedule was all over the place and I acted like he wasn't there for his daughter. I told James to calm down, that no one was saying he was not there for Deshaun. What I said was that this was her freshman year in high school and she would be attending college starting in the summer, and she had dental appointments and therapy appointments. I needed him to help me pull some of this weight. I was not a single mother and I should not feel like one either. He said oh okay, I got you. I can do that, I will step in. I said thank you.

As time went on, Deshaun's therapist suggested that she be reevaluated, and she referred us to a psychiatrist. I did not tell James about this appointment because I was very exhausted arguing with him about her treatment plans. It seemed like he was in denial and I just didn't have it in me to constantly argue with him about it anymore. So I took her on my own, and the psychiatrist diagnosed Deshaun with depression and anxiety. She also prescribed her medication therapy. I had all intentions of telling James that I had allowed Deshaun to take the medication, but I wanted to have a face-to-face meeting with him because those conversation seemed to go over better.

Unfortunately, I did not have the opportunity to talk to him because when I wanted to talk with him, he told me that he was going away soon, and we would talk when he returned. I agreed, but before he left, Deshaun called her dad to pick her up from school and ask if she could stay the night. He picked her up and while they were in the car on the way to his house, she remembered that she needed to get her medication from my house. So she asked James to take her home before they left, he said for what Deshaun, I can wash your uniform tonight. She said because she had to get her medicine. At that point he responded, "Medicine! What medicine?" She explained that it was the medicine that her psychiatrist had given her to take. He was confused and asked, "Your *psychiatrist*? What do you mean your psychiatrist?" Deshaun told James that I had taken her to see a psychiatrist the other day and she had given me medicine to take. James could not understand why Deshaun needed to take medicine so Deshaun explained that she had been diagnosed with anxiety and depression. James answered, "Anxiety and depression? You don't have no anxiety and depression! There is nothing wrong with you! You don't need to take no medicine. What are they trying to say, that you crazy? You ain't crazy, ain't nothing wrong with you. You are just becoming a teenager. And your emotions and hormones are getting the best of you. You don't need no damn medication! I don't agree with you taking medication.

Deshaun sat there and didn't say one word. She was hurt and didn't understand why her dad never stopped and thought about her feelings. She said he just went into a rant and didn't stop. I ask her how it made her feel and she said honestly mom I was sad because dad never once asked me how I felt about taking medication and if it would help me. He didn't ask me anything and honestly he made me feel like I was crazy. I knew he was upset because I didn't tell him, but this was her life. I asked her if she wanted to take the medication and she did not know. She didn't know what to think anymore. Does taking this medication really that mean that I'm crazy?

Deshaun asked me what I thought. I reassured her that she wasn't taking medication because she was crazy, but because her doctor had recognized that there was a chemical imbalance that she couldn't control; her emotions were either really high or really low—almost like a roller coaster. I began to give her common analogies that she could easily identify with.

I explained to her that her dad had high blood pressure right. She said yes. OK, so his doctor prescribed him medication to regulate his blood so his heart didn't have to work so hard. That didn't mean that her dad was abnormal; his medication was regulating what his body couldn't control on its own. She was like, oh OK. I see what you're saying Mom. I said here's another example. My father had diabetes—when one's body has a hard time breaking down the blood sugar. My dad was prescribed insulin which acted as a regulator. It actually helped his body to break down the sugar in the blood. So just like a person that has high blood pressure. Your dad, and a person that has diabetes. My dad a person couldn't always look at someone like them and tell that they were struggling with something.

Just because Deshaun had been diagnosed with anxiety and depression and was prescribed medication, did not mean that there was something wrong with her. It just meant that she needed this medication to help to regulate her thoughts and emotions so that she could function with a clear head and be the best Deshaun that she could possibly be. No one could look at her and tell that she had been diagnosed with anything. There was nothing wrong with her; this was not something that she had and it certainly does not define who she is. This was something that she was experiencing. Taking medication did not mean she was crazy. There are a lot of people that we see every day who are diagnosed with anxiety and depression, and we would never know it. That's probably because they are taking medication to help to regulate their thoughts and emotions so that they can function and have a good quality of life. Deshaun just looked at me with a smile on her face and told me that she was really glad to have me as her mom because I understood her. I smiled and said I am too baby.

When she told me how James had reacted when finding out that her psychiatrist had prescribed her medication, I was furious! I could not wait to get James on the phone. I was ready to give him a piece of my mind. I could not believe that he had the nerve to say such harsh things to my baby, as if she didn't have feelings. When I called him, I just cut straight to the chase. I ask James what possessed him to go off on Deshaun when she told him that she was taking medication. He asked, what do you mean? I told him how she shared with me the conversation that they had the other day while she was in his car. And how he expressed to her all of his personal thoughts and feelings regarding her taking medication.

Did he not think that his reaction was too severe or that it was inappropriate? He was like, well first of all. You didn't tell me that you were taking Deshaun to see a psychiatrist. And secondly, you didn't tell me that Deshaun's psychiatrist was putting her on any medication. I acknowledged that I intentionally did not share that information with him before taking her to her first appointment. It was because I was tired of arguing with James about Deshaun's treatment—why she has to go and what went on with her therapy. James never picked up the phone to ask how she was doing or how her therapy was going. I had to make sure that she had everything that she needed because James was not supportive of her care.

Did he realize how exhausting it was going around the horn with him? Therefore, I decided that it was best that I made the decision to take her to the appointment and have a conversation with him later. That was what I was going to discuss with him before he told me that he was going away. He insisted that I still should have told him. I agreed but added that he should have been able to understand why I didn't say anything to him before. He said well I mean I guess I can. I ask, can you really understand. I asked him to put himself in my shoes. I was sitting here taking her from appointment to appointment and trying to explain to him or keep him abreast of what was going on with Deshaun and he gave me friction at every turn. This was exhausting. *I was the one who was walking these floors at night. I was the one that was talking to her and comforting her in moments of distress.* He was *not* the one that was dealing with these things. How did he think I felt going through this by myself? How did he think Deshaun felt when she was sitting there listening to him go off on a tantrum about his disapproval regarding her taking medication? Does he know how she felt? Did she express to him how his words made her feel? Did he even know the impact that he had on her when she was sitting in his car and he was having a total meltdown about something that she was experiencing? I bet he hadn't even thought about that. He should have because she expressed to me that he hurt her feelings. The things that he said to her made her feel like he didn't care about her.

And she was confused about her decision to take the medication even though she knew that it would help her focus. Here I was, having to clean up the mental and emotional chaos and destruction that he caused. He couldn't go off the deep end just ranting about his personal feelings. He should have tried to put himself in her shoes, imagining how she felt. It was not right. I told him that he had to be very careful about how he expressed his thoughts and emotions. He could have his feelings about the situation, but he should have expressed his thoughts, concerns, and feelings to someone else; not to Deshaun.

He became very quiet on the phone, and finally he apologized. He recognized that he owed her an apology because he probably should not have said those things. He just wished that I would've called and told him that I was considering taking her to see a psychiatrist and agreeing to her take medication. I agreed and understood his point of view. My question to him was what would it have changed if he knew earlier? Would he have been on board with Deshaun being reevaluated? He didn't think so because he didn't think that psychiatric treatment was necessary. I interrupted him and explained that the very reason that I didn't tell him was because I could not go back-and-forth with him about the quality of care that our daughter clearly needed. If the physicians felt that the medication was not needed or was not the best option for her, they would not have prescribed her anything. He agreed but still insisted that he didn't see any purpose for medication because there was really nothing wrong with her. I agreed with him— however, this was something that was going to help her to be able to focus and continue to do well in school as well as any other areas of her life. I needed James, as her father, to be on team Deshaun. This was not about me and this was not about you—this was about Deshaun. So I asked him if I could count on him to support whatever Deshaun needed. He agreed.

Within the next few months I asked him occasionally to take her to both her therapy and psychiatry appointments, and in the beginning he did well. There was no hesitation and he seemed to be on board with her care. I thought we were making good progress, until I happened upon an email one day to discover that I received missed appointment invoices from both offices. I had no idea he had not taken her to her last four appointments. We discussed the dates and he even went as far as putting them on his calendar so that he wouldn't forget. I had no way of knowing that Deshaun didn't go because she stayed at his house during those times since it was more convenient for him to take her. I was pissed!

So I screen shot the images and sent them to him in a text. He called me and tried to act like he didn't know what he was looking at and I explained to him that he had to pay those missed appointment fees, because he was responsible for taking her. Also, there was a scheduled appointment that I knew nothing about, and he swore me up and down that he didn't make that appointment. I knew that he was lying because I knew the scheduling process so well. The nail in the coffin was when he told me that he would have taken her to the appointment because he was off anyway. No shit, sherlock. That's how I knew he had scheduled that appointment. He complained that he didn't have the money at the time to pay for any missed appointment fees. I told him he had to figure it out because it happened on his watch. He had the nerve to tell me that since Deshaun lives with me, she was my responsibility. Say what! He said you heard me. I told him okay, you got it buddy. No worries. She was my responsibility, so he didn't have to worry; I would take care of it. And then I hung up the phone.

I was hurt and in total disbelief, because the James Tolson that I know would have *NEVER* in a million years said anything like that to me or about our girls. I had a conversation with my boyfriend about it and he said, baby, maybe James was going through something at the time. He reminded me that James worked a lot and he may have been overwhelmed. I took what he said into consideration, but it did not sit well with me at all. I pondered my boyfriend's explanation for months, and it really drew a wedge between me and James. I became distant and didn't call to ask him for his help with anything.

The fact that James did not agree with psychotherapy broke my heart because *clearly, he of all people needed it the most.* Why didn't he reach out to someone? Why didn't he seek help? Quiet voices whispering messages in our ears. They are speaking to us in the dark places. In the moments of solitude the silence screams our secrets. It magnifies our fears and inefficiencies which fuel the catalyst that result in the commission of suicide. We are not a perfect people but we allow the embarrassment of our actions, decisions, and circumstances to hold us captive. Because of this we keep ourselves bonded and in constant submission to our guilt. Thus the manifestation of internal anguish and the misconception of no escape.

Even if he didn't want anyone to know that he was seeing a therapist, we hand delivered his help. He did not have to worry about the pressure of finding someone to talk to because I had already done the research. It would have been easy for him to backtrack and speak to either Deshaun's therapist or her psychiatrist without anyone knowing if embarrassment was one of his concerns. Did he think it would affect his career? That could have been a part of the reason. As a law enforcement officer, his career relied greatly on his mental, emotional, and physical stability; so it could have been difficult to reach out for help. The fear of opening up and talking about what was eating him up deep down inside could have been difficult to face. It wasn't an easy decision to make, so often law enforcement officers masked what they saw and how they felt from day to day. They moved with the notion that just talking to someone about how they truly felt and the things that they were going through could possibly take away the very thing that gives them life: *their career*.

James buried himself in his work, not because he had to but because he needed to. He was not very financially responsible and for that reason found himself in one hardship after another. He walked around encouraging others as if he himself was not in pain and didn't do the thing that mattered most. He should have just reached out. It was hard to talk about the dark side of his thoughts—and in his field of work, he knew that if he revealed his true feelings—these thoughts, the ones that guided his final decision—then drastic measures would have needed to be taken. I believe it would have and in fact they should have been taken. Perhaps we wouldn't be remembering James and he would be here to receive the helping hand he so often gave to others. It is sad that society does not embrace mental health in law enforcement. It is almost drilled into the officers as a "BOLO" (Be on Lookout). But as we all know, there isn't always a sign, or a cry for help. Sometimes the red flag is a gunshot to the head. How do you make peace with that? How did we fail James? He did not fall short of happiness in his life. He was going to propose to his lady in the coming days, his grandson and daughter were coming home for a season, and his birthday was just five days away. And despite all the joy that surrounded him, he felt that his internal pain was so great that the decision to take his life was the solution. This was pain that not one of us knew about or even thought was eating away at him.

Our family is not alone on this journey, this has become an epidemic. In this year alone, the police suicide rate across the country is growing rapidly. There are so many reported cases of police suicides every week, and it seems that very little intervention, if any, occurs. How often is anyone checking in on our public servants? The military is supported so greatly for PTSD, but it seems that police officers aren't considered in the same capacity. They should be. It isn't always the stress of work that could push someone to the edge; *police officers are people, too.* They break, they hurt, and sometimes it is hard to heal. It is easy to assume that they are okay without actually asking them. And I know firsthand that they aren't from some of my personal experiences as a police officer. The sad reality is that sometimes they don't know it themselves.

I remember when I was on the force and I was going through my divorce. I didn't realize that it was affecting my job until my sergeant referred me to see a therapist. When I sat in that office and spoke with that man, he asked me one simple question—and that question made me weep like a baby. I didn't know that I was suppressing so many emotions and above all, feelings of depression. I think we hide from the word *depression,* as if it is a death sentence. In reality, as a common cold if depression is treated properly, it will yield a successful outcome. You don't just wake up depressed—something happens to trigger this mental and emotional tug of war. Some tragic experience may affect you so deeply and make you feel like you are losing control. It is different from day to day and quite honestly, from moment to moment. Depression is often paired with anxiety and sometimes you can turn it off. But most times, it becomes so overwhelming that you just can't function. However, no two people experience it the same.

Perhaps in James' case, his was an overwhelming sadness because he expressed sadness a lot. The girls had told me that their dad had been very tired in the last few months and didn't seem to have the energy to do as many of the things he enjoyed. Deshaun expressed that James was a little snappy and becoming very distant. She even expressed feeling a disconnection of some sort. I know this to be true because she had not stayed the night over his house in two weeks, and she was either always at her dad's house or wanting to go over. Even if it was to stay one night it didn't matter to her, as long as she spent time with her daddy. And it didn't matter to him either because he would work a double shift and pick her up so tired and wake up early to take her to school. That was the kind of daddy he was. There was nothing he would not do for those girls; they were his pride and joy. Everybody knew that his girls were his everything, and he wouldn't have it any other way. If he was proud of anything, it was being a dad.

CHAPTER SIX

Daddy's Girls

Tyler, our oldest was not his biological daughter, but you would never know unless we told you. He came into her life at very tender age, right before her second birthday. Although her father was in her life, he stepped into those shoes and took the bull by the horns. He was there every step of the way; he attended every school event and volleyball game. He wanted to capture every moment of her life because he didn't have children of his own when we met. He fell madly in love with her from day one. I remember the day that she called him daddy for the first time, we were sorting ornaments in our new home and this was right after we had gotten married. She looked at him and said in her sweet voice, "Are you going to help me put the angel on the tree, daddy?" We both stopped in our tracks and looked at one another and she looked him in his eye and said, "Daddy, are you going to help me?" I just nodded my head at him with a faint smile and he lifted her from the floor and raised her to the top of the Christmas tree and surely, she put the angel in place. I could tell that his heart skipped a beat in that very moment, to hear her call him daddy radiated in a big smile. From that day on, there was nothing he wouldn't do for that little lady. I even taught him how to put her hair in a ponytail. Now that didn't always work out, but the effort was everything. Seeing the way he loved my baby made me fall in love with him. It was like God chose the perfect person to hold her hand through life and he did just that. She could always call on him. When she held daddy's hand for the father-daughter dance at her sweet sixteen, it was James that she chose, and it was James that loved her first.

Tara, our middle daughter was James' biological niece. Her mother was his youngest sister, who died when she was very young. James' biological mother was instrumental in raising her until her death shortly after. At the tender age of seven, she came to live with us because James would not have anyone else raise her. She was going to be placed in foster care and when he learned of this, he came home and asked me if she could come and live with us. He could not bear the thought of her living with anyone else. It wasn't a thought in my mind to see her anyplace else. So without any hesitation, I agreed to have Tara live with us. For many years, we battled in court while caring for her and James' sister Dominique didn't make it an easy process. Every time we had to appear in court, she appeared in court. She tried to do whatever she could to have Tara removed from our home because she thought we were doing it for the money. Little did she know that the $162 James received every month was nothing in comparison to the structure, love, and stability we were able to provide for her. As the days went by and the years rolled on, she was no longer our niece—she became our daughter and we saw her no differently.

Our sweet baby Deshaun was a gift from God. Before Tara came to live with us, Tyler asked for a baby sister. I knew that it was almost impossible for me to have more children, so I told her to ask God for a baby sister. And she did; every night as she said her prayers, she asked God for a baby sister and every morning while I was doing her hair, she rubbed my stomach and said, "My baby sister is going to get in your belly, mommy." I just smiled and asked her if that is what God told her. She said with confidence yup it's going to happen. I think James planted that seed because he always talked about us having a baby, and for years we tried. After much medical advice, we finally conceived. When I told him that I was pregnant, he picked me up and spun me around; he was thrilled! Then he needed to sit down. He was so excited that he could not stop smiling. He said I am going to be a daddy. Tears began to fill his eyes and trickle down his face. When I asked him if he was he crying, he quickly wiped his face and said No girl!. I teased him and said okay, you were just sweating from your eyeballs, and we laughed.

When I gave birth to Deshaun, our little bundle of joy, James almost passed out. Afterward, he wouldn't let her out of his sight. He was such a proud daddy. He always showed people photos of the girls Everywhere he went and took them to his job on his off days. There were coworkers that he was close to that became aunts and uncles to the girls. He was a real teddy bear about his little ladies, and it never changed throughout the years. So, when the girls felt what we didn't know then was actually a shift, we can now see it clearly when we reflect on that time during James' life.

Now that James is gone, and we come together both family and friends, the days grow long, and the sun doesn't seem to rise. It is hard to go about our days knowing that he is no longer with us, and it is even harder knowing that we will never hear his voice or his laugh. That he will never pick up the phone or call us just the same. We will never see his face or hold his hand and the memories are all we have to hold on to. As this reality sink in and I sat in this chair, I am reminded by my mother's embrace that this too shall pass, and the healing process will be slow. I lay here full of emotion, but mostly full of fear. I don't know if I can answer all of the questions or ease the pain of my children. Although I lost my friend, they lost their dad and that feels like everything. I pray that God strengthen me to be a comfort for them. I pray that he give me the words in perfect time to render a little peace, but mostly I pray that they seek God for comfort of healing their brokenness.

My mommy prayed with me and over me, and she assured me that I was not alone. I wish that her words would have penetrated me more deeply because that was exactly how I felt. *Alone.* I told her that my partner was gone and here I sat all alone to carry the weight of being the backbone for our children. I expressed to my mother what a tough pill it was to swallow—and being the main support system for my children. My mother reassured me that I was not alone. I had so many people in my corner and that they were all here for me and the girls. I continued to lay there and as the tears streamed from my eyes, I still felt helpless. It was late and I needed to rest, because tomorrow was going to be as challenging as today.

When I got home, I called each of the girls to check on them once more for the night. I could tell that they each were just as exhausted as I was, but Deshaun was a little more upbeat. Perhaps going to her godmother's house was best for her, and that put my mind at ease a little. I did ask Tyler and Tara if they wanted to join me in the morning at the funeral home, and they both agreed. I was relieved because I did not want to do this alone, and I felt it was too late in the evening to call Natalie. So, I took a nice, hot shower and went to bed. I didn't rest well at all—I kept seeing flashes of James' face from the last time I saw him and then of the bathroom in his house. I must have jumped up a dozen times wishing that this was a nightmare. I was trying to shake it off but I couldn't. I just lay there for hours until daybreak and finally, I had to get up and get moving. I sat on the side of the bed gazing out of the window, feeling so tired and stressed thinking of how to start this day. I called Deshaun to check on her and to see how she was feeling. I wasn't sure if she was going to want to go to school or stay home, but I needed to hear her voice before I decided how to start the day. I asked her how she rested and she told me she had just fallen asleep about two hours ago, so I decided that she should stay home. When we got off the phone, I called Tyler and Tara to wake them up so they could get dressed to meet me at the funeral home and then I got moving.

CHAPTER SEVEN

Preparations

I was standing in the bathroom looking in the mirror as I brushed my teeth when a rush of emotion came over me. I looked at the mirror into my eyes and said to myself aloud, *you can do this.* I took a deep breath and turned on the shower. As I stepped in, I felt a brisk chill on my shoulders; I had an eerie feeling come over me and my shoulders felt really heavy. As the water messaged my back, I held on to the wall, held my head down, and began to cry. I could not help but think about the moment that James pulled that trigger. I could see it clearly; it was like a movie playing in my head. I imagined the pain he was in and how scared he had to have been at that moment. I knew that this was not easy for him and I was racking my brain to understand what he could have been going through to follow through with this.

Damnit, James! Why did you do this? I asked myself this question constantly. A part of me wished that he would have whispered the answer in my ear or came to me in a dream. And then the reality kicked in—that I would never know—and perhaps he didn't want me to know. Then I became angry. How could he selfishly do this? How could he make the decision to take himself away from our girls like this? What the hell was so bad that this was his best option? I just didn't understand. But it wasn't for me to understand; I just had to accept it. I am not sure how much time had passed but I needed to get a move on it. So I got out of the shower and sat on the side of the bed and took a deep breath once more. I needed to call Natalie before I go to this funeral home and see if she wanted me to pick her up or if she wanted to meet me there. When I picked up the phone to call her, my phone began to ring. It was my mom, calling to say good morning and find out if I needed her to accompany me this morning. I let her know her that I was fine and that the girls were meeting me there. I told her that I was going to call Natalie again and ask her to come as well. My mom prayed with me before we got off of the phone. I called Natalie's and there was no answer;, the line just rang and rang. I disconnected the call. I did not want to leave a message because I had so much to say and I felt like a message was so impersonal.

I continued getting dressed and called the house again when I got in the car. Natalie was so fragile and I knew that she moved in slow motion, so I wanted to keep trying to reach her because I wanted her there. I really wanted to honor her wishes for her son, but the line just rang. I did not stop trying to reach her. I called once more when I arrived at the funeral, just before I walked in. Again, no answer. I felt uneasy about this. I really wanted her to be there. I wished that there was some way that I could speak to her, but after the way that Devlyn acted yesterday, I knew it was best that I did not go to her house unannounced. So I was left no other choice than to proceed without her.

While we were sitting in the waiting room, we were told that Mr. Grier, the owner of the funeral home, was coming to meet with us himself. While we waited, I had to excuse myself to the restroom because I was emotional and did not want to upset the girls. They were doing so well at the time. When Mr. Grier arrived, we were escorted to the conference room and the first thing he asked was how we were. He understood that James was a police officer, and it was his privilege to serve our family. Mr. Grier spoke so warmly, and he made us feel like family. He gave us his undivided attention and he treated us with honor and dignity. That was so important to me, especially because of the nature of James' death. When you speak of suicide, people become very critical and judgmental and they speak without consideration of loved one. So it made us feel very comfortable with our decisions to select this funeral home.

Talking through the options went well until we had to discuss the details. This is where having Natalie there would have made a big difference, so I took a moment and called her again. If I could have her on the phone, maybe she could give me some insight on what direction to go. But again, there was no answer. I was really disappointed that no one was there to help us, no one from his family called me at all. It really took me by surprise because no one knew that I was arranging services for James and it became clear to me that no one from the family had so much as called to take care of him. What were they waiting for? Why did it seem that I was the only one who cared enough to put him away? It didn't make sense at all and it was strange, because there is nothing that James would not have done for his family. I don't know if everyone was holding out to see who would volunteer to step up, but who has time for that.. It's not as if the medical examiner's office would hold on to his remains forever, so what were they waiting for?

At any rate I must press on. Here is where things became challenging for me. I had attended several police officer funerals and every experience was very different than the average service. Originally, I thought that this was going to be a state-wide service with hundreds, if not thousands of officers from many agencies in attendance. So it was essential to have his services in a church that could accommodate everyone. But I had to speak with Michelle to confirm these details before making any decisions. I must have called Michelle every day for one thing or another; she was my saving grace.

Next, I had to select where he would be laid to rest and I tried to think of the best place for his family so I thought of where his dad was laid to rest. Unfortunately, because his dad served in the military and James had not, that particular location would not be possible. So, I put that on hold as well. As we progressed with the arrangements it became increasingly difficult. I tapped out and asked the girls what they desired for their dad. It was becoming increasingly exhausting trying to consider what someone wanted in their absence and more importantly, despite my attempts to reach out to James' family members, I was met with silence. I decided to move forward in the best interest of our children. It did not seem fair to them that they walk through this journey alone and have to stand by for someone else's wishes to be considered. I chose to put them first. I really wanted their input; he was their father and they should be the ones to say what they wanted for their dad. Besides, I was grateful that things worked out the way they did because I was able to make sure that Devlyn did not do to my girls what she did to James when his father died.

The hardest and most overwhelming part was when we had to pick out the casket. We had no idea that the showroom was adjacent to the conference room where we were seated. When Mr. Grier opened the doors it was incredibly shocking to our systems. When we turned around, we all stopped in our tracks as if our feet were stuck in position. I am not sure if they were waiting for me to walk through first, but I could not do it. I just could not walk through those doors. I turned away and placed my hand over my heart as I supported myself at the table with my other hand. After talking about the cost of the service, I was in no way ready to walk into this room with caskets.

Mr. Grier comforted us by telling us that he understood that this was a difficult part of the process, and we could take all the time that we needed. I nodded my head as a gesture of gratitude, but I could not bring myself to even look in the direction of that room. I did not want to do this, but as I was trying to gather my emotions, Tyler and Tara were falling apart as well. I took a deep breath, wiped my tears, and pulled some Kleenex from the box on the table. I walked over to the girls and gave them the tissue and held them both in my arms. I told them that I knew this was hard, but we could get through it. Here I was, in my broken state, and just the sight of my children hurting snapped me right back into mama bear mode. I had to be strong for them so that we could pull through this. I held both of their hands and we walked through those doors together. I turned to each of them and ask if they were alright and they both answered yes.

I told them to look around and let me know if they saw something they wanted. As they walked around on one side of the room, I was perusing the other side of the room. One of the things that stood out to me was cost. Caskets were expensive! I was shocked at the cost and I was more stunned when I discovered I was looking at the lower price range. Tyler and Tara, on the other hand, were not looking at price but style. It was no surprise that they wanted a $10,000 casket. At first sight I was looking at the style and color. The style was nice, but the color would not compliment his clothing. I wanted James to be honored so I decided that he would wear his dress blue uniform. We discussed complementing colors and when it came to price, I told the girls we had to make another selection. We did not have an insurance policy and because I was paying for everything, I did not want to go over the budget I had set in place. So we went over to the other side of the room where I had originally started and selected a really nice casket. I suggested some really nice embellishments similar to what the girls selected on the other casket.

Now that we had those difficult details taken care of, I was ready to go. Mr. Grier had called Pastor Scott at Shuber

Baptist Church to ask him if we could have the funeral service there, because he knew that the church would be large enough to accommodate a funeral of this magnitude. I was so grateful and blown away because he really went out of his way to guide us through this process. While we were there, Pastor Scott called and he agreed to host the services for us. Finally, I could see things fall into place. I was beginning to feel like this was a good sign of things to come. When we left, I had to finalize the remainder of the details by speaking with Michelle and selecting burial arrangements. Once I had this done, everything would be all set. I talked with the girls briefly before leaving the funeral home and asked them how they were feeling and if they needed anything. I wanted to check in with them periodically to make sure they were okay.

I went to my mom's house which was around the corner from the funeral home, and I sat and talked with her about the things that we put in place. She asked if I had spoken to Natalie and I told her that I had unsuccessfully tried to reach her all morning. She wondered why Natalie wasn't answering the telephone to which I said that I would not be surprised that my number was blocked after the way that Devlyn behaved yesterday. It wasn't like Natalie to ignore the telephone, so this had Devlyn written all over it. I wasn't going to put too much energy into that situation because I had enough on my plate. My mom felt that I should not have had to make all of these arrangements alone. I agreed but reassured her that the girls had helped me make decisions.

I was so surprised that no one called to check on the girls. *Not one single person called to see how they were doing.* They had just lost their dad and no one wanted to call to see if they needed anything. The hell with me, I didn't expect a phone call but I have had the same number for thirteen years and not one person thought to call and see about the girls; a damn shame. It's sad actually, imagine how they feel. For years, his family acted like they loved the girls so much and embraced them with open arms. It made me think that it was all for show. It was so strange that no one—not Devlyn or Uncle Ronald—had stepped up to take care of James. If someone in the family had actually called, I would have been notified because the medical examiner would have told them that James had already been moved. If I were them, I would have wanted to know where James was and who had made the decisions going forward. Either they didn't care or they were relieved that someone else was doing it. That's why I decided to make the girls' wishes my priority and help them honor their dad. My mom was so supportive and offered to help me if I needed it. I was so grateful for her and hugged her.

I called Michelle to iron out the details for the service. I wanted to know what the department's plans were, and she told me that she would get back to me with that information. It didn't take her long to call me back, and to my surprise, she said the agency was not giving any input for the services. I asked what she meant by they weren't giving any input for the services? and she said that because of the way James died; he forfeited a complete police funeral. This meant that there would be no acknowledgements, no mourning bands, no flag presentation to the family, no honor at the cemetery, and no honor guard ceremony. I said are serious! So You mean to tell me that this man put on that uniform for over twenty years to serve this city and because he died by suicide he is stripped of all honors? How disgraceful is that! As his wife, I sacrificed my husband every day knowing the possibility that he may never walk through that door again, and my children sacrificed their dad not knowing if every day would be the last day they got to love him. And now he gets nothing! This was completely unacceptable; for all we know, the stress of his job could have been *the very reason* we were here. It's like he was here today and gone tomorrow. How in the hell was this okay? I needed to talk to someone about this. Michelle said that she understood how I felt but there wasn't anything she could do.

I sat on that phone and my heart broke into a million pieces. I knew the feeling of putting on that uniform and saying a prayer of protection over myself for God to bring me home to my family safely every day. The thought that none of that mattered to them was heartbreaking. This may only have been a job to his superiors but for James, he sacrificed *everything* for the City of Baltimore. And now they just washed their hands with him in the end? Michelle sat silently on the other end of that phone and listened as I poured out my frustrations to her. I knew that this was not her decision, but it hurt to know that James was treated like trash. She was so understanding and finally said that she would see if she could do anything. She would make a few phone calls and get back to me. She didn't want to make any promises, but would try her best to see if there was something she could do. I didn't have much more to say but I thanked her through my tears, hung up that phone, and was bursting with frustration—I let out a belting scream.

My mom quickly came in the room to see if I was okay, she ask me baby what's wrong are you okay, and I just wept. I told her that I couldn't believe that the Baltimore City Police Department would not allow James to have any honors at his funeral because he committed suicide! She said what! Are you serious! I can't believe this,. The least they could have done is honor his service, but it seemed that protocol had no mercy for that. *To protect and serve, for what?* If you didn't live or die by the guidelines, then your service was conditionally appreciated. I don't care how he died! James gave so much of himself to that damn department down to the minutes before his death. I was so glad that the girls were not here when I had that conversation because they would have been devastated, and I did not want to tell them one more thing to upset them.

In the days and weeks to follow, I was able to finalize everything for the funeral. I selected a cemetery that was not far from where we all lived so that the girls would not have to drive far to visit their dad. When I met with Rich, the cemetery associate, to select the burial site, they offered me a preselected plot. I initially thought this was going to be easy, but it was the complete opposite. Rich told me that he would guide me out to the location and if I was pleased, we could come in and finalize the contract. We each got into our vehicles and proceeded to the preselected sight, which was right around the bend. As Rich walked me over to the plot, I noticed that it was not too far from the road. That was a plus for me, because it would be easy to find when the girls came back to visit.

We got out of our cars and walked a few feet over. I stood there for a moment and looked around. I don't know exactly what I was looking for, but for some reason I could not say yes. It seemed that this was more difficult than I thought. Why couldn't I just say yes? To be honest, for me this was just a business transaction, but to my girls, I knew that it was much more. So, I asked Rich if I could call my daughter to see if this was a good location for them. I didn't feel right making this decision; in fact, I did not feel right making any decisions. For a second, I wished that Natalie was here because she would have the final say, but that was not an option, so I called Tyler. She was at work, but the perk of working for your mom was that she was able to leave and meet me. A few moments later she arrived, and I asked her what she thought about the location. She looked around and became very emotional. I felt guilty for dragging her there to make such a decision, but I was not thinking about the moment. I was simply pressing my way to the end. I walked over and held my baby in my arms and thanked her for being so strong.

In that very moment it came to me, and I knew what I had to do. I looked at Rich and asked him if there were any available plots in the Tranquility Park, and he said he would check. We waited while he called into the office and I told Tyler she could leave. She had all that she could take for the day and I would work out the rest. Rich escorted me over to the Tranquility Park and when I walked over to the open plots, I knew I made the right decision.

A few months ago one of Tyler's friends (now my son) Jayce lost his mother and she was resting in the same place. I remembered from attending her services, that it was peaceful near the lake and beautiful with the fountain on. I also knew that Tyler had accompanied Jayce often when he visited his mom and I thought it would be suitable for them to support one another. So, I selected a plot that was right above hers. It was perfect. I will say that I did not like the cost, but it was a small price to pay for peace. During the completion of the contract, Rich showed me options for the gravestone, and I told him that I wanted the girls to make that selection as well.

Saturday morning we met at the cemetery and went over all of the options. You would think that these girls was signing checks and taking names. They wanted everything they saw. One wanted a memorial bench, one wanted the largest tombstone, and the other wanted an angel with wings statue, and not one of them asked for a price. I was sitting there looking at them like they were crazy. I asked Rich for the price range for their wishes and he politely informed me that neither of them could go in that location and we had to select one of the plaques. I was so relieved to hear that because I had already spent enough money and this was the last check that I planned on writing.

The options for the plaque were nice. They selected a nice ribbon banner to go under his name and his department badge on one side with his photo in the center. It was laid out very well, but Rich told us we needed to have a crystal-clear photograph or it would not turn out well. We scanned through some photos we had and he told us that they were not quite good enough, so I asked him if he needed the phot to begin the process. He assured me that they would wait for the photo so that they can process everything at the same time, and he asked if I could bring it in Monday. . I told him that I would look through what we had and let him know if we were able to locate one and he said that would be fine. I asked him if I could get the check I wrote the other day for the plot so that I could write one check for everything and he told me that they already transacted on that check. I asked him if he would wait until I brought the photo back before he processed the check and he assured me that he would wait.

Now that everything was in place, the last thing I did before calling Michelle was to go to James house and get his dress blues and take them to the funeral home on Monday. But for now, I needed to rest. After leaving the cemetery, I realized that for once, I did not have a telephone call to make or an appointment to keep. It was the first time that I didn't need to do anything. On the way home, I stopped to grab something to eat; I didn't want to be bothered with cooking. I got in the house and nearly undressed at the door,

I showered, and slipped into my jammies and indulged in the best meal I had eaten in a few weeks. It wasn't long after my head hit the pillow that I was out for the night.

Monday afternoon, I decided to go to James' house and pick up his uniform so I could take it to the funeral home. And you would not believe the shit I walked into. The locks on the front door were changed! That damn Devlyn changed the locks because we didn't give her the key! I called Michelle to see if there was anything I could do about it, and she regretfully informed me that the department could not get involved with family domestic issues. I knew her fat ass was probably sitting back laughing like she did something slick, but I bet she didn't see me coming. I called Dominique and told her to go to the courts and become the custodian of James' estate so that she could take possession of the house and then I called a locksmith and changed the locks myself.

When I gained entry into the house, I attempted to clean up the bathroom. After three hours of scrubbing, it was impossible to break it down because the blood and tissue had been there for so long. So I had to schedule a biohazard service to come over. I called to request a quote and I was told that they could not give me an absolute price without seeing the scene. There was a $500 deposit for them to come out. The company representative told me that the minimum payment would start at $1,500. I knew right then that I had done all that I could do. I was in no way going to pay that kind of money for a cleaning service, but what was alarming to me is that Devlyn supposedly loved her brother so much that she put forth no effort to clean it herself.

I gathered his uniform I needed for the funeral and locked the house up. I didn't have time to be playing games with this childish woman. My brother was getting married the following week and I needed to have everything in place by the close of business Tuesday.

I confirmed everything with Michelle and was pleased. But as the business of things dwindled down, we were experiencing a lot of hardships and setbacks. The girls were struggling by the hour. Deshaun was in no condition to attend school and she was sinking further and further into depression. I was so worried about Tyler who could not control her emotions and she, too, was falling into depression. And Tara became very distant because this is how she dealt with grief. I found myself being pulled in so many directions and aimlessly feeling my way from minute to minute. My words were few and my thoughts were scattered when handling everything. I became so overwhelmed I began to reach out for help. I needed to seek assistance for my girls because they were suffering so much.

I was referred to Roberta's House for grief counseling. It was located in Baltimore City and they provided service for families, individuals (adults and children) who had lost loved ones; they provided healthy healing through their grief. I reached out and it took a while before they called me back; I had to call a few times and as they say, "The squeaky wheel gets the oil." I set up the date for us to start therapy. Originally, we were scheduled to start in December and I remember thinking what a long time to wait for therapy. But I was willing to do whatever it took to get us through. In the days to come, I would talk with the girls about how they were feeling, and I gave them journals and suggested that they write daily. I told them that they should write letters to their dad about their day. Just because he was no longer here, it didn't mean that they couldn't carry him through their lives. I told them to start their entries with, "Dear Daddy today" and whatever they experienced or thought throughout the day; to share it with him. Although he couldn't respond, this was their way of sharing your life with him as if he was here.

This seemed to work well for them, but they struggled occasionally. I would ask them if they had written lately. They got really quiet and said no. . I ask when was the last time you journaled. They would say it has been a while. I encouraged them to journal and just like clockwork, they magically felt better. Sometimes it was hard to believe in the process. Healing wasn't easy. It didn't always make since, but journaling was important for healing. As I am standing as antecessor for my children I am taking a beating. We are being tormented by Devlyn and her Daughter with threats of violence via social media. Devlyn came to my home while I was not there, and I felt that I needed to protect my family. So I found it necessary to go to the courts and file a restraining order against Devlyn and her daughter Penny to ensure that my children were safe while I was out of the country.

On Wednesday morning, I headed to Mexico for my brother's wedding and I made arrangements for Deshaun to stay with her godmother for the week. I thought that I finally had an opportunity to unplug from everything. I was so wrong. As I was standing in the baggage claim, I turned on my cell phone and it nearly jumped out of my hand. There were so many messages that came through that I couldn't check to see who it was. The messages were pouring in from everyone. Tara sent me at least six messages containing screenshots of conversations between her and Dominique. The funeral home was trying to reach me, and Mr. Grier himself was trying to reach me as well. I wondered what could possibly be going on because everything was in place before I left. That was short lived. Where do I start?

Tara and Dominique argued because Dominique told her family that I made the arrangements because I had the policy, and Tara defended me. The funeral home called because Devlyn had called Pastor Scott and cursed him put for allowing me to have James' funeral services there without her permission. So Pastor Scott refused to allow us to have the service there. Mr. Grier called me because Devlyn told him that she was going to sue him and have his business shut down because James and I were divorced and I had not spoken to him in years. She chastised him but was willing to allow me to move forward with my plan as long as the family reviewed the program before it went to print.

After speaking with Mr. Grier, we were well within our rights to move forwards since Deshaun was next of kin and I was her representative. I spoke with Deloris from the funeral home regarding Pastor Scott and she advised me that she had two options to pursue and asked which option I preferred. One of the options was my home church and she expressed that she had already reached out to her bishop. What do you know we fellowship at the same church! I told Deloris that I wanted to move forward with our home church. I called Michelle to update her of the chaos and she advised me that Pastor Scott was so nasty with her when she called to schedule the walk through for the department. I was flabbergasted! How in the world did everything that I worked so hard to put in place unfold in a matter of hours? I spent the first three hours in Mexico on the phone troubleshooting. I was putting out fires everywhere. After some time, I was able to restore some order.

Dominique with her sneaky ass—instead of signing the documents to give the funeral home permission to move forward with the arrangements that I made—tried to get access to the bill. When they wouldn't give it to her without my permission, she flaked out on them. I tell you, vultures will stop at nothing to cause havoc. Why won't they just sit down and shut up. One would think that James' family would be thankful that I was paying for *everything*. Dominique was on a rant with Tara and told her she was going to throw James in the oven because she didn't have any money to bury him. And this came from the people that supposedly loved James dearly; carrying on like a pack of wild banshees—such animalistic behavior from the people he called family!

The most difficult thing for me was doing the right thing, and I know my faith was challenged at every turn. I wanted to say the hell with it all, step back and let everything go because I was so frustrated. But I knew that if I did that, then what was most important would have been lost. And my focus was putting James to rest with dignity and honor. I battled lies—by James' girlfriend who accused me of breaking into the house and stealing her engagement ring. That backfired on her quickly because I had already been in Mexico for two days when this supposedly happened. I wasn't surprised when she testified at the hearing that she was James' fiancé. Now which one was it were you engaged or was he going to propose? Either way I didn't give a shit because it was not my business, but she was so fast to jump into the fire with them. She paraded that morning like a scorned woman, but she surly didn't call my phone to take over. I would have gladly handed the torch over to her. I had been talked about and disrespected from day one by people who wouldn't know me if I had walked past them or even spoke to them. They were upset with the idea of who I was. I knew that James had said some horrific things about me to a lot of people. But we all knew that hurt people hurt people. He surely never imagined that I would ever come face to face with any of those he confided in. While these people only heard the song of a scorned man, they told themselves stories that they believed were true.

Cast judgement because they attach emotions to someone they know absolutely nothing about. None of this bothered me because I knew this going in. I knew that James did not deserve all of the effort I put when I walked through this remarkably challenging journey, and he certainly was not worthy of the hardships that I endured. But for my girls, I would have walked through fire. Believe me; I walked through this fire for them. I knew that in life, we must know when to rise to the occasion and remain above the chaos. It didn't mean that the road wasn't tough, or the journey easy, but we had to have purpose in everything that we did.

So I held my head high and I moved in silence, because to do it any other way was beneath me. I was a woman of integrity with dignity and class., and it takes so much more than rumors and the opinions of others to knock me down. I realize that the business part of this process was easy but the emotional part was a true struggle. There were times that I wanted to defend my emotions and there were times that I just didn't care. It was hard for me to accept that I was entitled to every thought and feeling that I experienced. It was okay to be sad, confused, upset, and even angry. As I positioned myself to be emotionally and physically available for my girls, I was happy to have a village of my own. I needed them more that I could ever imagine. I knew that I would not have made it through without them by my side. I was grateful for every telephone call, every supportive ear, and every word of advice, because without them I would have folded. They allowed me to be vulnerable and cry, they kept me accountable to my faith, and they gave me strength to just breathe; they were ready to go to war on my behalf. James' Aunt Pat, whom I loved, got my number and called to check in on us from time to time. She and Uncle Ronald's wife were very helpful by stepping in and represented the family for me; I really appreciated them.

I decided to schedule the funeral two weeks away because James' wound was to the head and I wanted to give the funeral home time to prepare him for services. It was important to me that he looked as close to himself as possible. I wanted everything to be perfect for the girls.

Since Tyler and I went to court the very morning of the viewing to handle the Devlyn and Penny situation. They had filed countersuits against us while we were out of the country so we had to deal with that. The judge was very clear and fair. She expressed that we all suffered a loss and no one won in this case. Deshaun was the most important person in this matter because she had lost her father and we needed to come together as a family for her. After all was said and done, neither Devlyn nor Penny attended the viewing or the funeral.

Michelle told me that she would arrive at the funeral home early. I called her when we arrived and she met us in the parking lot. She asked me if I wanted to allow anyone to come in with us during the family hour and I said no. I wanted the girls to have their time uninterrupted with their dad. I wanted this vulnerable time to be private for them. So I asked if she could hold anyone that arrived outside until they were ready. While we were there, Deloris came over to talk to me about the program before it went to print. She asked me if I wanted to put Devlyn's name in the obituary. Every fiber in my being wanted to tell her no, so I did. But Deloris hit me where it hurt: she told me that she realized I had been through a lot with Devlyn, but the Bishop had challenged you to stretch your faith and you are being stretched. So she asked me as a woman of God and her sister in Christ, what I wanted her to do. I stood there with tears streaming down my face and rage running through my body and told her to add her name.

I hated doing the right thing. Why did I always take the beating and be held accountable to doing what is right? I was so angry but my heart knew that once again, I had to make the right decision. As Deloris walked away I heard a loud thump outside. I looked around wondering what that noise could possibly have been. Michelle was standing at the rear of the chapel and she approached me and said that the honor guard had positioned themselves to come in and post. My heart melted and I hugged her so tightly. I wasn't expecting them to be there. I don't how this was possible; perhaps because my heart was in the right place God granted me mercy. I was so thankful for this honor, everything was perfect.

My girls finally got to see their dad honored as he should've been. We were asked to stand aside as they marched in. One after another they rendered a salute to his lifeless body laying front and center of the chapel. The last officer on the honor guard stood post at a forty-five-degree angle at the head of the casket. The American flag was at post and he stood still as the doors opened and everyone came to pay their respects. I stayed until the girls were ready to go after the funeral. I was pleased that everything was just as I imagined it would be.

Michelle walked me to my car and as we embraced and she acknowledged my successful efforts of organizing the funeral. She said, "Well done Tarsha, you did an amazing job and I am so proud of you." She encouraged me to get some rest and would see me in the morning for the church service. Before I laid my head to sleep that night, I thanked the Lord for favor and peace. I know that He carried me all the way.

CHAPTER EIGHT

The Last Call

Saturday, September 28, 2019. I awoke in prayer.

Dear God, thank you for waking me up this morning. I have done all that I can do, and I pray that you are pleased with my work. My faith was tested, and my body is tired, but I ask that you strengthen me on this day. As we gather to bid James farewell, I ask that you surround us with perfect peace and protection from ill wills and let no weapon formed against us prosper. I pray that your will is done and all I ask you to do is give me the strength to hold my head high just one more time. In Jesus' name I pray, Amen.

I had been praying for everyone so much that today I needed pray for myself. I woke up the girls to get ready. I called everyone that was coming to my home to made sure they all were on schedule, and I prepared myself. The funeral director arrived and as we assembled in the living room as he prayed over our family. We gathered our last-minute things and proceeded to the church. As we traveled the expressway, the billboards alerted everyone that there was a police officer funeral procession to take place today. Deshaun asked if the signs were for her dad and I said yes baby they were.

When we pulled into the parking lot my eyes opened so widely because I could not believe what I was seeing. There were Baltimore city police cars staged everywhere. The motorcade was assembled and as we were waiting to exit the family car. Police officers aligned both sides of the vehicle at the doors and escorted us into the church. I was overcome with emotion. We assembled in the lobby and the family that was there waiting for us filed in position right behind us. We were then escorted into the sanctuary individually to view James and then escorted to our seats.

After the family came, then the command staff and the officers from his district filed in. Dominique walked down with her entourage and sat on the opposite side of the isle from where we were seated. She walked up to the casket and practically laid on him. She started with a moan and the more she moaned the more attention she got. She cried out, "That's my brother! Jimmy, why did you do this?" And her entourage gathered around her; one began to fan, the other grabbed the Kleenex, and the other two were posted behind her, just in case her legs decided to give out. It was a spectacle to observe. As they motioned her to stand and turn to her seat, she threw her head back and her matted wig smothered the lady that tried to hold her up. I almost burst out laughing, but I just snickered. No sooner after she sat down and everyone moved from in front of her, she jumped up from her seat and extended her arm to shake the hand of every person that approached the casket. It was another spectacle. She thanked them for coming and carried on as if she was his widow. I just looked at her and shook my head. When the service began, she occasionally cried out, "Oh Jimmy, what am I going to do without my brother?" She sat there rocking back and forth bobbing her head up and down, all the while not a tear in her eyes. She was in full character the whole time. I was happy when the Reverend began to preach, because all of the foolishness stopped and his message was amazing. The eulogy was powerful. The service was beautiful.

Surprisingly, the girls held up well, struggling here and there. The most difficult time for them was the closing of the casket, but that was hard for everyone. Deshaun did not want to see that part so she excused herself and my niece accompanied her to the restroom. Tyler and Tara stayed in their seats but they both looked away, and I held their hands as the funeral director lowered his head and finally closed the casket. Deshaun returned to her seat just as the family was escorted outside of the church. The officers positioned the girls and I in front of the family car which was approximately two car lengths behind the hearse, and they stood alongside us as we waited. There were uniformed officers lined in formation on both sides of the hearse from the front to the rear, and the honor guard continued the formation to the family car.

The command staff exited the church and directly behind them was the Reverend escorting James as he was carried by his fellow officers. They walked in sync, carrying him slowly down the stairs and into the parking lot, and stopped directly in front of us. As they turned in the direction of the hearse, the honor guard called a salute, and each officer rendered a salute to James as he was escorted to the hearse for his last tour of duty. Although the assembly was small, the honor was grand.

Once James was secured in the hearse, everyone exited the church and we prepared to depart from the church for the graveside service. The motorcade escorted the hearse and we followed directly behind. The brigade of cars assembled in single file as we convoyed to the expressway. There were members of the motor unit positioned at the intersections to stop traffic in all directions as we approached, and they surrounded the entire convoy to ensure that no outside traffic disrupted our commute. The girls were looking through the rear window of the family car at all of the cars that were behind us. There were red and blue lights as far as the eye could see; it was difficult for us to see to the end.

As we made our way up Interstate 695, the traffic headed in the opposite direction was at a standstill. We saw people standing outside of their vehicles waving and rendering salutes as we passed them by. My heart filled with a thousand butterflies and tears welled up in my eyes to see the civilians of Baltimore honor this officer for his service. I pointed out to the girls all the people who were on the overpass standing with outstretched American flags, and waved us on. It was a beautiful sight. The commute was quite lengthy, and I was happy, because this gave us time to pause a bit. We listened to music and enjoyed some snacks in the car. We were prepared because we knew that it would be a while until we were able to eat, so I insisted that we packed some light snacks for the ride. Once we arrived at the cemetery, I told Devin that we would get back in the car once the service was over and wait for everyone to leave.

The girls and I walked over to his actual gravesite and watched them lower James into the ground. The girls wanted to have a private moment with their dad, and I wanted that for them as well. Once we noticed the people walking over to the canopy we began to exit the vehicle, and we were instructed to remain in the car. Shortly after, the honor guard assembled at the head of our car and formed a tunnel as the escorting officers aligned themselves alongside the vehicle. They opened the doors and assisted us out of the vehicle and proceeded to escort us to our sets in front of the casket.

As we sat there, the Reverend said a prayer and committed James to the ground. As he began to dismiss us, he announced if anyone wished to stay back and join us as we watched James lowered into the grave. We looked at each other in shock. I was furious because that was supposed to be a sacred moment for the girls only. I looked at them and nodded my head to eliminate any concerns they had. I instructed them to remain seated as everyone walked away. I looked over and saw Rich standing on the side and I signaled him over to me. When he came over I asked if he could wait until everyone left the cemetery before they lowered James into the grave and he said that was fine; he would wait for my signal to call the grounds crew over. That was a relief, and I instructed the girls to follow me into the family car while we waited for everyone to leave.

As we waited, not many people lingered behind, but I did notice Natalie walking towards a car. I exited the vehicle and called out to her. I waved the girls to follow me so that we could speak with her before she left. I called to her and she turned in my direction, as we locked eyes, she welcomed me with open arms. I hugged her and kissed her cheek and as she patted my back, she said you did good Latarsha. She thanked me for having taken care of everything—she knew I would because Jimmy had told her that if anything happened to him, that I would. She also thanked me for taking care of her son and then she told me she loved me. I hugged her so closely because during all the chaos and stress her words meant everything to me. The girls came over and hugged and kissed her as well. They all exchanged lovely sentiments and we escorted her to the car.

As she left the cemetery, we stood by waiting until we could no longer see her, and I signaled to Rich that we were ready. We stood in the road waiting for the groundskeepers to come over and we watched them lower James into the grave. The girls walked over to the car and I told them I would be there in a second. I stood there for a moment closed my eyes, took a deep breath, and as I exhaled you bet I gave him the salutation that I know he deserved. In my mind it went this way.

As we sat under the green canopy before us lied a hero, in a gray casket draped with the American flag in honor of his service. The honor guard stood post at each end of the casket. The Emerald Society stood in position on one side of the canopy near the lake and the firing squad stood at rest, posted on the other. The Reverend said the prayer and committed James to the ground. Next, we heard the bagpipes and drums playing *Taps*, the mourning song of the fallen hero, followed by the Three Valley Salute shots fired in honor of the deceased officer.

A few seconds of silence slowly coming in our hearing were fighter jets flying over in the missing man formation an aerial salute in memory of a fallen officer. And finally, the last call. The sound of a radio call: dispatch to Officer James Tolson H614... and silence. A few seconds later another call. Dispatch to Officer James Tolson H614... and again, silence. A few second later, the dispatcher acknowledged there was no response from Officer James Tolson H614. *End tour of duty.* Tears began to fall from my eyes and the honor guard raised the flag and commenced the folding ceremony which was a moving tribute of lasting importance to the officer's family. The flag was presented to the girls. This is the honor that James served for—he sacrificed days, nights, weekends, and holidays for the city of Baltimore and as I stood here, I wouldn't ever allow anyone take that away from him.

James Tolson II, born September 15, 1961—his end of watch was on September 9, 2019. So much more than an officer. He was a son, a brother, a husband, a boyfriend, and an amazing father in his lifetime.

As I turned and walked towards the family car empty handed because we did not receive a folded flag, I imagined how his final call would have gone. The telephone would ring with me answering. "Hey James, what's up?" And he'd reply with, "Hey Frank, you got a second?" And I'd say, "Sure what's on your mind?" And he would reply…

I will never know what *could* have been said, because he didn't want me to know. I can never imagine what *would* have been said because, I wasn't supposed to know. And I will never know what *should* have been said because, I never got the call. No matter the reason, James decided not to call. We make peace with knowing that he suffers no more; that his heart was big and he was gentle as an ocean breeze. We will carry his light in us, remembering his voice, his smile, his laugh, and the joy. Our family is broken but will learn to heal with the passage of time, we will remember him.

James, we will forever remember you.

CPSIA information can be obtained
at www.ICGtesting.com
Printed in the USA
LVHW051338171120
671905LV00007BA/192